The Past, Present and Future of Sustainable Management

Stephen Cummings · Todd Bridgman

The Past, Present and Future of Sustainable Management

From the Conservation Movement to Climate Change

palgrave macmillan

Stephen Cummings
Victoria University of Wellington
Wellington, New Zealand

Todd Bridgman
Victoria University of Wellington
Wellington, New Zealand

ISBN 978-3-030-71075-0 ISBN 978-3-030-71076-7 (eBook)
https://doi.org/10.1007/978-3-030-71076-7

This Palgrave Pivot imprint is published by the registered company Springer Nature Switzerland AG
The registered company address is: Gewerbestrasse 11, 6330 Cham, Switzerland

To Noelle, Maria, Caithi, Sierra, Oisín, Savannah, Leo and Zach

Preface

This book is about what might be the world's most important collective problem: Sustainability, or how can we ensure the healthy continuation and thriving of humankind and the natural environment. It is also about one of the world's fastest-growing academic subjects and practices, and one which may be applied to any other field: Management. And its time-span—the Past, the Present and the Future—is as broad as it could be. It is a lot to cover in a book of this size. We cannot provide comprehensive coverage of any of these things in a small volume, so we've made some choices about the best way to advance our argument.

We start by placing a marker in the present: the third decade of the twenty-first century; and outline some of the main historical assumptions that inform people's thinking about Sustainable Management now. We begin to question these assumptions by looking briefly at the pre-modern past. Then, more specifically, we examine the recent past of the development of management as a subject across the last 120 years.

Most especially, we zero in on the years around 1910 in the United States, the time and place at which Management, as a subject, is assumed to have been born, and where it is assumed that sustainability was the furthest thing from the key protagonists' minds. The hinge of our project here is that this is not the case: sustainability was at the forefront of the thinking of those who made Management. In particular, it was key for the person who becomes the book's protagonist: Louis Brandeis.

The counter-history we present argues that despite what the conventional history of Management tells us, it was Brandeis who first conceived of Management as a subject, or a unified body of knowledge. He defined the 'central motive' of this new field as 'conservation', or what we today might call sustainability. Only later would others formulate what has come to be the accepted view: that Management's fundamental good or end is economic efficiency. Another founder was identified who reinforced that view and Brandeis and his work became a footnote. Then it was forgotten.

The new history that we describe in this book rediscovers Brandeis as a key point of origin for Management. Our discussion of the past, present and future of Sustainable Management then extends back from Brandeis to the earliest indigenous societies, and forward towards new ways of thinking about Management for the future: new ways which place sustainability at the heart of our field.

Wellington, New Zealand

Stephen Cummings
Todd Bridgman

Contents

1 **The Presence of the Past** 1

1.1 The Second Biggest Problem of the Decade 1

1.2 Histories of the Present: A Foucauldian Approach 5

1.2.1 An Acknowledged Bias Against Conventional Histories 8

1.2.2 Critiquing Cumulative Continuities from Singular Points of Origin 8

1.2.3 Discarding Chronological Evolution and Juxtaposing Discontinuities Instead 9

1.2.4 Seeing Development as a Result of 'Problematizations' Not Continuous Evolution 10

1.2.5 Subjects and Objects Are Not Separate and Distinct, but Co-Created 11

References 12

2 **The Conventional History of Sustainable Management** 15

2.1 Management's Newest New Thing 16

2.2 The Good and the Origin of Management (and How Sustainable Management Does Not Fit) 21

2.2.1 The Good of Management 21

2.2.2 The Origin of Management 27

2.3 Sustainable Management: Child of the 60s, Adopted by Management in the 2000s 30

2.4 Second Thoughts 33
References 35

3 A Counter-History of Sustainable Management (or How the American Most Hated by Big Business Invented Management) 39
3.1 Efficiency Made Good 41
3.2 The Formation of Management as a Subject with Conservation at Its Central Motive 46
3.2.1 Management for Conservation 49
3.2.2 Management for Social Justice 55
3.2.3 Management for Economic Efficiency 56
3.2.4 Taylor's Embrace of the Good of Conservation 61
3.3 The Emergence of Brandeis's View of the Good of Management 69
3.3.1 Student, Practitioner, Teacher 69
3.3.2 Advocate for Better Management 74
3.3.3 Isaiah's Elevation: Management Guru to Political Prophet to the Supreme Court 84
3.4 Brandeis's Foundations Fade 87
3.4.1 A Fork in the Road 90
3.4.2 History Chooses Taylor as 'the Father' 93
3.4.3 Brandeis Ebbs Away 96
References 99

4 A New History of (Sustainable) Management 105
4.1 The Case for Another Origin 109
4.2 A New History for the Future 114
4.2.1 New History Part I 114
4.2.2 New History Part II 127
4.3 About-Face 138
References 141

Index 145

List of Figures

Fig. 2.1	'Management Perspectives Over Time' (Adapted from Samson et al. *Management*, 2021: 40)	19
Fig. 2.2	Three Pillars of Sustainable Development (Adapted from Schermerhorn, *Management*, 2020: 140)	30
Fig. 3.1	Newspaper advertisements including the word 'efficiency' (Data from the ProQuest Historical Newspapers database)	44
Fig. 3.2	Number of times 'conservation' appears in front-page stories in major US newspapers (Data from the ProQuest Historical Newspapers database)	52
Fig. 3.3	"They All Want Mr Brandeis Now". Published in the *Boston Post*, February 26, 1911 (*Source* Mason 1946: 328 facing)	62
Fig. 3.4	Frederick Taylor's draft of an introduction to *The Principles of Scientific Management*. Stevens' Institute F.W. Taylor Archive (Box 59, file 20b)	65
Fig. 3.5	"Thus Perish all Patricians". Published in *The Boston American*, May 24, 1908 (*Source* https://brandeiswatch.wordpress.com/2012/05/04/editorial-cartoons-of-louis-d-brandeis/)	83
Fig. 3.6	"The Blow That Almost Killed Father". Published in *New York World*, January 29, 1916 (*Source* https://brandeiswatch.wordpress.com/2016/02/04/editorial-cartoons-about-brandeis-supreme-court-nomination/); "Scandalized". Published in *The Los Angeles Times*, January 30, 1916 (*Source* Mason 1946: 595 facing)	88

Fig. 4.1 Founder of management: Frederick Taylor vs Louis Brandeis 110
Fig. 4.2 The United Nation's Sustainable Development Goals. Reproduced with permission 137

CHAPTER 1

The Presence of the Past

Abstract In 2021, the Covid pandemic dominated the news cycle. But the global issue that was gaining traction before Covid struck, sustainability, is not going away. As Covid fades and we seek to redouble our efforts to promote Sustainable Management, one unrecognized obstacle we face in Management Studies is the belief that the focus on sustainability is a new phenomenon: rather than a continuous human concern that was overlooked as Management evolved in the 20th century. As a means of interrogating this belief we propose the 'counter-historical' approach of Michel Foucault and outline how we shall apply this to thinking differently about the historical development of Sustainable Management.

Keywords Sustainability · Indigenous Peoples · Sustainable Management · Michel Foucault · Counter-History

1.1 The Second Biggest Problem of the Decade

Before Covid there were the fires. Beginning to write this book in Australia in December 2019 you felt them closing in. They started to

S. Cummings and T. Bridgman, *The Past, Present and Future of Sustainable Management*,
https://doi.org/10.1007/978-3-030-71076-7_1

subside as the pandemic hit, and at the beginning of 2021, as we finalized the manuscript, the fires seemed distant. But they will burn again, and will continue to burn after the worst of the virus has been tamped down.

There is a song about Australia called *This Land is Mine*, sung as a duet by Kev Carmody and Paul Kelly.[1] It is an insight into a critical dichotomy in Australian history and society: one that mirrors a similar tension between modern colonizers and indigenous peoples around the world.

The first verse is Kelly describing a white settler's experience, tirelessly working his portion, improving his asset, trying to get ahead. 'This land is mine', he sings. The second verse, by Murri indigenous musician Carmody, voices a different relationship with the same place—a place referred to by Australia's First Peoples as Country. The capital C signifies that Country is a being, of which Carmody is a part. It envelopes and is one with him. It does not belong to him, or Kelly, or the bank that lent the money to Kelly to buy it either. Carmody's refrain is 'This land owns me'.

Perhaps the most promising innovation in how to manage the fires in Australia, California and other parts of the world, is an attempt, by some, to re-appreciate the pre-modern knowledge that Carmody's lyrics represent (Steffenson 2020; Cowan 2020). The recent Victorian Traditional Owner Cultural Fire Strategy, developed in partnership with the Victorian State Government and the Australian Government's Department of Environment, Land, Water and Planning, is an example of that.[2]

In the strategy's words—"it is becoming increasingly acceptable as a practice for public land managers to involve Aboriginal people in land management activities" (VTOCFS 2019: 4). That it was not previously thought to be acceptable to involve the people who lived in Country for thousands of years, is a result of modern history-making.

Prior to 1788, the people of Country used cultural burning practices in a highly sophisticated way to manage landscapes: burning sections of land when appropriate to enable sustainability. They used these burning practices for a wide range of purposes:

[1] Paul Kelly, Kev Carmody and Maireah Hanna, 'This Land is Mine', from *One Night the Moon* [soundtrack], MusicArtsDance films, Sydney, 2011.

[2] 'The Victorian Traditional Owner Cultural Fire Strategy'—Victorian Traditional Owner Cultural Fire Knowledge Group, 2019. https://knowledge.aidr.org.au/media/6817/fireplusstrategyplusfinal.pdf.

- environmentally they sought to protect Country and sustain the beings within it;
- burning also promoted the social fabric that brought people together in associated work and rituals;
- economically, it enabled the sustainable harvesting of necessary food and other resources; and
- culturally, burning was connected to art, myth and traditions passed through generations.

Subsequently, the people of Country "approach[ed] land management with a holistic set of practices that link the management of conservation and productive values to the environmental and cultural services on which they depend" (VTOCFS 2019: 20).

When Europeans arrived in Australia, this approach was misunderstood, dismissed as archaic (and preposterous), filed as a curiosity in the annals of history, buried and forgotten: replaced with a modern focus on securing and protecting the assets in order to maximize short-term financial gain. It is hard to believe that there is not an element of racism in dismissing an approach not dissimilar to other cultures ideas about crop-rotation (the waru, or fire, paintings of Minyawe Millar of Karalamilyi River, which can be found online if you search for them, provide a good illustration).

The VTOCFS strategy explains how this marginalization has created a "huge gap" in our knowledge of the management of Australia/Country. Furthermore, "departure from cultural burning practices after European colonization has resulted in significant and detrimental changes to biodiversity and has inadvertently <u>increased</u> risk to life and property from wildfire" (VTOCFS 2019: 20, underlining added).

In short, fire or waru in Australian ecology was traditionally a partner, an element in the solution to how generations may live in balance with Country. The colonizers made it the problem and it is this problem that we are waging an increasingly costly war against every wildfire season. The VTOCFS strategy begins with a simple statement: that "Fire is healing"; and then seeks to outline the ways in sharing knowledge about how to use "the right fire for Country" and the achievement of "culturally meaningful objectives", will also "achieve risk reduction as a complementary objective" (VTOCFS 2019: 4).

The example of how the first people of Australia worked within and developed their relationships with Country, is an illustration of how sustainable management can be seen to have existed for thousands of years. An illustration of how the past of this field is much deeper than we commonly assume.

∞

Perhaps the biggest selling book of the past decade advocating sustainable management, Naomi Klein's (2015) *This Changes Everything*, captures how the history of Sustainable Management is generally viewed: management discovered sustainability a few decades ago. And, "for a quarter of a century", Klein (2015: 26) explains, "we have [subsequently] tried the approach of polite incremental change, attempting to bend the physical needs of the planet to our economic model's need for constant growth and new profit making opportunities". But the friction between the environment and business interests has reached a never before seen peak, so that it is now a never before seen existential crisis, where growing environmental interests directly "conflict with the fundamental imperative at the heart of our economic system: grow or die" (Klein 2015: 21).

We seek to look at the same issue and problems that Klein and others have identified, but with a broader historical perspective. Both sustainability and the conflict between management from a capitalist standpoint and environmental and social issues have been around for a lot longer than the past few decades. We would claim that the impact of modern colonizers clashing with indigenous peoples, was in many respects a greater collusion than the one *This Changes Everything* focusses on. But, because indigenous peoples did not have a voice in the creation of written history, we have tended not to recognize this. But, we will argue, going back further to look at sustainable management may enable us to think in ways beyond the 'incremental change' that disappoints Klein and other modern commentators.

While beginning this book with the story of two approaches to land management: modern and pre-modern, is a good way into an alternative history of sustainable management for the future, we are no experts on indigenous practices. That exploration is better left to people who are.

Instead, we will try and open up further space for such a re-appreciation by focussing in on an area that we do know more about. Our area of inquiry is the period and culture around which the subject defined as management studies emerged: the first decade of the twentieth century. This is where the "fundamental imperative at the heart of our economic system", of which Klein writes, is generally regarded to have emerged. It is where the growth of a new industrial world in the United States encouraged the creation of modern management and its earliest theories.

What we will highlight in looking deeply into this period runs contrary to the conventional history of Management and sustainability too. We will find that the subject we know as Management was born as environmental and economic interests confronted one another. They clashed in a way similar to the tectonic, 'this changes everything', collision that Klein sees in 2015. And the solution to this clash was named to be conservation—a solution that we might give a more modern term today: sustainability. The imperative, at the outset, was not 'grow or die'. It was conserve thoughtfully so that we may live better for longer.

Consequently, we will argue that sustainability was not just at the heart of pre-modern existence. It was there at the heart of the development of modern management too (How we forgot this is an interesting story, one that we will explore in Chapter 3). Recovering this history can help us to think differently about Sustainable Management, and Management generally and encourage substantive rather than just incremental change in the present.

This argument will require undoing a lot of conventional history, recovering old history and creating new history. So how, exactly, will we go about doing this?

1.2 Histories of the Present: A Foucauldian Approach

In *The History of Sexuality—Volume 2: The Use of Pleasure*, Michel Foucault articulated an approach to history that he had been developing for decades. His work, he explained, (1985: 9) sought to:

> learn to what extent the effort to think one's own history can free thought from what it silently thinks, and so enable it to think differently.

This book presents three histories of the present toward its aim of thinking differently about the past, present and future of Sustainable Management.[3] These are:

- the conventional history of Sustainable Management (Chapter 2);
- a counter or alternative history to this (Chapter 3); and,

[3]Throughout the book, when we seek to denote a subject such as Management, Economics or Sustainable Management, we capitalize the terms.

- a new history that may provide a basis for thinking differently (Chapter 4).

The arrangement of these three different histories helps define the book's philosophy and approach. The philosophy, broadly speaking, is that all histories are reflections of the times in which they were written. Their aim may be to tell us some truth about the past but they also tell us a lot about the values and beliefs of the people who wrote them, those they were written for and the purposes for which they were used (Nietzsche 1957; MacMillan 2010). They are, in this way, cultural artefacts. Like a hemline or a style of painting, each history reflects the context in which they have developed.

The first of our three histories is the present history that records what is generally regarded as how current ideas about Sustainable Management came to be.

The second is an alternative history, informed by the re-thinking of conventional histories that is becoming prevalent in a widening range of fields, from psychology to international relations, and which some call a 'historical turn' in the social sciences (Klein 2017). This seeks different points of origin and other lines of development, by looking critically at the formative events in their own contexts, rather than in hindsight.

Inspired by the juxtaposition of our first two histories and their illustration that history can be thought otherwise, our third history aims to think more freely about Sustainable Management's historical precedents in a way that can more readily enable substantive innovation for the future of management.

In arranging our project in this way, we are guided by the work of 'counter-historian' Michel Foucault. Foucault is hard to pigeonhole. He might be variously described as a philosopher, sociologist, anthropologist or ethnographer. He wrote histories from all of these angles, but he was not a historian in the conventional sense. Foucault (1985: 9) described his projects as "studies of 'history' by reason of the domain they deal with and the references they appeal to; but they are not the work of a 'historian'".

The historian that Foucault does not wish to be confused with is a scholar who writes history in a Hegelian manner: uncovering the truth of events, the theses and anti-theses of past periods, and presenting them as a chronological chain of progress in a linear way. A chain that leads to or causes our present higher level synthesis. For this kind of historian, events or causes not seen as contributing to our current achievements are glossed over or edited out. This adds up to a history of 'winners', where past events, while seen as separate from the present, are believed to be linked in a cumulative sense, and this 'chain' is built in terms of present circumstances.

For Foucault, what this type of history does, sometimes unwittingly sometimes with purpose, is legitimate or add credence to the present establishment. Foucault (1985: 9) claimed that "instead of legitimating what is already known", his goal was to know how and to what extent it might be possible to rethink the history of conventional historians and enable thinking otherwise in the present and for the future.

Further insight into what such an approach entailed is provided by Foucault's own entry (written under the pseudonym Maurice Florence) on 'Michel Foucault' in the *Dictionnaire des Philosophes*. Foucault suggests that his works be referred to as "critical histories of thought" and that these are neither histories:

> of the acquisitions of truth nor a history of its occultations. [Instead, I write] the history of the emergence of truth games. It is the history of 'veridictions', understood as the forms according to which discourses capable of being deemed true or false are articulated within a domain of things: what the conditions of that emergence have been; what price has been paid for it, as it were; what effects it has had on the real; and the way in which, linking a certain type of object with certain modalities of subject, it has constituted for a time, a space, and particular individuals, the historical a priori of a possible experience. (Florence—a.k.a. Foucault, in Gutting 1984: 314)

Hence, Foucault proposed that the histories of conventional historians are part of the 'truth games' that create the objects and subjects that we assume to have a real 'objective' and ahistorical existence. It was these histories and their limiting effects that he sought to question.

Subsequently, Foucault used conventional histories, and the assumptions they promoted, as starting points that his work would unravel by showing them to be part of a web of contingent relations. Foucault's own studies then engaged in a 'recurrent dialogue' with these conventional histories to produce 'counter-history' (Noujain 1987), or what Foucault (1977b) sometimes called 'effective history'—histories that would challenge established assumptions. The two histories, the conventional and the counter, side-by-side, created uncertainty and the space for new possibilities.

Foucault developed different approaches for doing this with different emphases and different names (e.g., Archaeology, Genealogy, Interpretive Analytics—Burrell 1988; Cummings and Bridgman 2011; Dreyfus and Rabinow 2014). But five general themes run throughout his work that we can utilize here to counter the conventional history of Sustainable Management in order to think differently for the future.

1.2.1 An Acknowledged Bias Against Conventional Histories

Foucault insisted that no history can give the complete or objective story. Given the dispersive nature of events and the multiplicity of lines of explanation between them, there is always a "polyhedron of intelligibility", and, subsequently, many ways to represent history, each with its own biases (Flynn 1994: 38). "Historians", wrote Foucault (1977b: 156–157) channelling Nietzsche, "take unusual pains to erase the elements in their work which reveal their grounding in a particular time and place [all] the unavoidable obstacles of their passion". They "invoke objectivity, the accuracy of the facts, and the permanence of the past [and] hide [their] singular malice under the cloak of universals".

In contrast, Foucault's historical sense would be "explicit in… acknowledg[ing] its system of injustice. Its perception is slanted, being a deliberate appraisal, affirmation, or negation [of] the history of the present" (Foucault 1977a: 31). Thus, Foucault never claimed to reveal the whole truth in his histories, but rather to raise doubts about what historians promoted as the truth of an object or subject's evolution. In a similar vein, we are clear at the outset that our targets are the conventional historical understandings of management and sustainability, and the ways in which they limit our thinking by encouraging incrementalism and building upon established foundations, rather than substantive innovation.

1.2.2 Critiquing Cumulative Continuities from Singular Points of Origin

Conventional histories tend to look back with hindsight to seek out 'present needs at the origin', then outline a 'progress of consciousness' from that point upwards, culminating at our present heights (Foucault 1980: 70). They present history as the identification of essential kernels of truth that define what a subject or object is about and then chart progress from there (Foucault 1977a: 142). Foucault's counter-histories sought to unsettle these conventional points of origin and the consequent evolution of knowledge drawn by historians by "dissolv[ing] the relationship ordinarily established between the eruption of an [origin] event and necessary continuity".

For example, the history of Management written in the second half of the twentieth century looked back and saw Frederick Taylor's Scientific Management as the earliest important study relatable to the essence of what management was understood to be at that time, and then plotted the progress of management knowledge from that origin, upwards and onwards. Since those histories were written, others have updated them adding the most recent discoveries, such as the importance of sustainability, to the end of the chain of progress.

Such histories, Foucault claimed, become 'the site of truth' and make 'possible a field of knowledge' by defining what it is about; but this 'truth' becomes "the sort of error that cannot be refuted because it [has been] hardened into an unalterable form in the long baking process of history [as it is constantly repeated]" (Foucault 1977a: 144). Sixty years on, those histories of management have been reiterated so often to have become unquestioned common sense, and this now limits innovation. We attempt to dissolve some of the assumptions on which such historical bases rest.

1.2.3 Discarding Chronological Evolution and Juxtaposing Discontinuities Instead

Foucault's (1977b: 160) explicit counter-historical bias against established origins and the continuities of progress presented from their starting points, led to the third characteristic of his work: the development of 'counter memories' through "a transformation of history into a totally different form of time". This involved moving from chronological time as an organizing schema to spatial juxtapositions that highlighted sudden discontinuities as opposed to a gradual evolution of thought.

Consequently, Foucault often juxtaposed quotations to highlight startling differences in ways of framing thought that have been conventionally overlooked or smoothed over. For example, in *The Order of Things* (1970: xv) a Chinese encyclopaedia's categories set against Western sensibilities in the same period, illustrate "the exotic charm of another system of thought [which is at once] the limitation of our own, the stark impossibility of [our] thinking *that*". In *Discipline and Punish*

(1977a), he began by presenting the description of a man punished by being publically tortured to death, next to an excerpt from just a few years later of a prison timetable that described punishment achieved via the discipline of a mundane drudgery behind closed doors. How, Foucault's counter-history of punishment proceeded to ask, did things change so much, so quickly? This could not be an evolution of understanding about the best way to manage punishment. It was an eruption that we have smoothed over in order to satisfy ourselves that our knowledge is cumulative and progressive. A particular eruption that Foucault set out to re-examine.

Such unconventional artefacts placed side-by-side, could open a window through which one might begin to probe our knowledge's forgotten predispositions. Similarly, we shall begin Chapter 3 with two quotations that highlight how it was a sudden and specific new way of thinking that created what we came to consider Management's universal good or aim.

1.2.4 Seeing Development as a Result of 'Problematizations' Not Continuous Evolution

This focus on sudden discontinuities where conventional historians see evolution and continuity, meant that Foucault needed to specify an alternative rationale as to why things changed or developed, rather than by a logic of the natural progress of thesis, anti-thesis and synthesis. Hence, Foucault's (1985: 10) counter-histories sought to reveal how transitions occur with shifts in "the conditions in which human beings 'problematize' what they are, what they do".

For example, some of Foucault's (1965, 1975) most well-known counter-histories showed how psychology and the human sciences emerged with the arrival of an age beyond that in which sovereigns could maintain control by 'doing violence' to transgressors. This shift created a problem of how social control could be upheld by other means. This problem spurred the development of the human sciences and their outlining of human norms and laws of behaviour that should be adhered to and which could be policed. By a similar token, Foucault's (1980) *History of Sexuality* outlines how people in the nineteenth century became interested in understanding and managing reproduction and sexuality as urban populations swelled, seeing the rise of new subjects like population ecology and the codification of sexual norms.

Our counter-history will similarly seek to raise doubts about conventional understandings of development. Doubts about the view that Management emerged naturally as part of the evolution of industrialization and our greater understanding of the importance of efficiency, by highlighting the particular, now unrecognized, problematization that spurred the emergence of Management as a subject in the first decade of the twentieth century: conservation.

1.2.5 *Subjects and Objects Are Not Separate and Distinct, but Co-Created*

Relatedly, rather than the perspective taken by many historians, that the objects that people studied have always existed, while the subjects or sciences that study them emerged later, Foucault saw objects and subjects co-determining one another. He argued, for example, that the species 'Man' as we understand him now, did not exist until the practices constituted by the rise of humanism and the human sciences took hold (Foucault 1970); and that what we define as 'madness', could not be conceived without the conditions that enabled psychology (Foucault 1965). An example of this, and an assumption that we shall counter later on in this book, is a claim that some management histories make that the object of management is as old as the Egyptians (although they did not, according to the same historians, properly understand it) while the subject Management emerged much later, in the modern era.

Foucault's histories were different in focussing on how subjects are not later developments, maintained and elevated not through their fidelity to the truth of the objects they study. Rather, they are given power by the knowledge networks or scaffolds that support them. These webs of political interests spread out to produce what we regard as knowledge and over time marginalize or dismiss other ways of knowing (other ways such as the traditional knowledge of indigenous peoples with which we began this chapter). These networks are increasingly obscured and become harder to discern, as secondary sources reproduce initial historical interpretations as universal facts. Uncovering them requires looking prior to the erection of these scaffolds, going back to examine artefacts at the time of inception, rather than relying on later interpretations and reinterpretations of what happened.

In keeping, our counter-history will look at how from the second decade of the twentieth century those concerned with the development of Management as a subject would define the object of their field in a way that was very different from the intentions of those who saw its purpose as advancing environmental and social goods. They responded to a different problematization: how to make Management seem to be a legitimate and popular subject for their times, defined the universal good of Management as economic efficiency, and created the conventional history of the field that has obscured Louis Brandeis and the Conservation Movements' presence.

∞

We are not the first to think critically about how Management's history limits development, or to apply Foucault for this purpose. There is a growing literature that probes aspects of Management's historical conventions (e.g., Hatch and Schultz 2017; Rodgers and Payne 2014; Rowlinson et al. 2014; Godfrey et al. 2016), and Foucault has been used to interrogate a number of Management subfields, theories and themes (Cummings et al. 2016; Scott 1987; Zald 1996). However, while inspired by these works, we seek to utilize Foucault's aim and approaches in this book to examine something different, something specific and something broader: both the history of Sustainable Management in particular and how this sits within our conventional understanding of Management as a whole.

In the next chapter, we begin by outlining the conventional history of Sustainable Management, identifying the accepted points of origin, and continuities from those points, upon which assumptions about the subject's development are based. This will be the target for Chapter 3's counter-history that spreads out from a juxtaposition that illustrates a forgotten discontinuity, and highlights the problematization that gave rise to an alternative origin of Management and its object, an origin of which we are no longer aware. Chapter 4's 'New history of Sustainable Management' (and Management generally), then encourages thinking differently for the future.

References

Burrell, G. 1988. Modernism, postmodemism and organizational analysis 2: The contribution of Michel Foucault. *Organization Studies* 9 (2): 221–235.

Cowan, J. 2020. Alarmed by scope of wildfires, officials turn to Native Americans for help. *New York Times*, October 7. https://www.nytimes.com/2020/10/07/us/native-american-burning-practices-california.html.

Cummings, S., and T. Bridgman. 2011. The relevant past: Why the history of management should be critical for our future. *Academy of Management Learning and Education* 10: 77–93.

Cummings, S., T. Bridgman, and K. Brown. 2016. Unfreezing change as three steps: Rethinking Kurt Lewin's legacy for change management. *Human Relations* 69 (1): 33–60.

Dreyfus, H.L., and P. Rabinow. 2014. *Michel Foucault: Beyond structuralism and hermeneutics*. Chicago: University of Chicago Press.

Florence, M. 1984. Foucault, Michel, 1926. In *The Cambridge companion to Foucault*, ed. G. Gutting, 314–319. Cambridge: Cambridge University Press.

Flynn, T. 1994. Foucault's mapping of history. In *The Cambridge companion to Foucault*, ed. G. Gutting, 28–46. Cambridge: Cambridge University Press.

Foucault, M. 1965. *Madness and civilization—A history of insanity in the age of reason*. New York: Random House.

Foucault, M. 1970. *The order of things: An archaeology of the human sciences*. London: Tavistock.

Foucault, M. 1975. *The birth of the clinic*. New York: Vintage.

Foucault, M. 1977a. *Discipline and punish: The birth of the prison*. London: Allen Lane.

Foucault, M. 1977b. *Language, counter-memory, practice*. Ithaca, NY: Cornell University.

Foucault, M. 1980. *Power/knowledge: Selected interviews and other writings, 1972–1977*. New York: Random House.

Foucault, M. 1985. *The history of sexuality: Volume two—The use of pleasure*. New York: Pantheon.

Godfrey, P.C., J. Hassard, E.S. O'Connor, M. Rowlinson, and M. Ruef. 2016. What is organizational history? Toward a creative synthesis of history and organization studies. *Academy of Management Review* 41 (4): 590–608.

Hatch, M.J., and M. Schultz. 2017. Toward a theory of using history authentically: Historicizing in the Carlsberg Group. *Administrative Science Quarterly* 62: 657–697.

Klein, H.S. 2017. The "Historical Turn" in the Social Sciences. *Journal of Interdisciplinary History* 48 (3): 295–312.

Klein, N. 2015. *This changes everything: Capitalism versus the climate*. New York: Simon & Schuster.

MacMillan, M. 2010. *The uses and abuses of history*. London: Profile Books.

Nietzsche, F. 1957. *The use and abuse of History*, trans. A. Collins. Indianapolis: Bobbs-Merrill.

Noujain, E.G. 1987. History as genealogy: An exploration of Foucault's approach to history. In *Contemporary French philosophy*, ed. A.P. Griffiths, 157–174. Cambridge: Cambridge University Press.

Rodgers, M.T., and J.E. Payne. 2014. How the Bank of France changed US equity expectations and ended the panic of 1907. *The Journal of Economic History* 74 (2): 420–448.

Rowlinson, M., J. Hassard, and S. Decker. 2014. Research strategies for organizational history: A dialogue between historical theory and organization theory. *Academy of Management Review* 39 (3): 250–274.

Scott, W.R. 1987. The adolescence of institutional theory. *Administrative Science Quarterly* 32 (4): 493–511.

Steffenson, V. 2020. *Fire country*. Melbourne: Hardie Grant.

Zald, M. 1996. More fragmentation? Unfinished business in linking the social sciences and the humanities. *Administrative Science Quarterly* 41 (2): 251–261.

CHAPTER 2

The Conventional History of Sustainable Management

Abstract A key element of Foucault's counter-histories is their explicit stance against conventional histories as a means for creating space for thinking otherwise about the past, and subsequently thinking differently in the present and for the future. This chapter outlines the conventional understanding of Sustainable Management's development as it is represented in Management textbooks. This history presents Sustainable Management as a new addition to the Management cannon. A breakthrough that has shallow roots and is hard to know how to treat because, unlike Management in general—which is understood as having economic efficiency as its fundamental good—Sustainable Management is about quite different beliefs, aims and goods.

Keywords Management · Sustainable Management · Economics · Efficiency · Triple Bottom Line

Foucault's work "culminated", wrote Gilles Deleuze (1988: 96), "in *The Use of Pleasure's* searing phrase: 'to get free of oneself'". And Deleuze's (1988: 119) description of Foucault's approach, which encapsulates this phrase, provides a useful way to think about this book's three histories:

S. Cummings and T. Bridgman, *The Past, Present and Future of Sustainable Management*,
https://doi.org/10.1007/978-3-030-71076-7_2

> Thought thinks its own history (the past), but in order to free itself from what it thinks (the present) and be able finally to 'think otherwise' (the future).

Our ultimate aim is a history of Sustainable Management that can help us to think otherwise for the future. We will get to that point by thinking of our own, new, view of Sustainable Management's past in the next chapter. But first, in this chapter, we outline the history of the present that we are seeking to free ourselves from.

Foucault's counter-histories targeted conventional historical understandings. Our target is the history of the relationship between management and sustainability, we outline this in three parts: first, we look at how Sustainable Management is presented as new and unprecedented in the annals of Management; second we examine how the good (or end) that Management aims to serve is understood to be very different from the good of Sustainable Management; and finally, we describe how Management is seen to have adopted thinking about sustainability that was first developed in the 1960s, 70s and 80s to create Sustainable Management in the decades after 2000.

2.1 Management's Newest New Thing

> *Compare a modern progressive, advanced company such as Google, which gives $5000 to its employees if they buy a fuel-efficient car and provides free unlimited food and many other benefits to staff at work, to the approach taken by generations of managers and business owners one hundred years ago, who often treated their workers as necessary evils.*
>
> Samson, Donnet and Daft, 'Sustainable Management and Management Thinking', in *Management* (2021: 60)[1]

This is a short book that requires taking some short-cuts. One is the utilization of the histories of management presented in introductory textbooks as proxies for the conventional historical perspective of Sustainable Management.

[1] This is the 7th Asia-Pacific edition of *Management*, which is a regional version of the 13th edition of *Management*, by Richard Daft. Both books share the same formats and generic content.

Despite a proliferation of pedagogical tools, textbooks remain the primary instrument through which students engage with a field (Kuhn 1970; Stambaugh and Trank 2010). And although they are accorded low status by some historians, textbooks are significant artefacts in creating and maintaining a subject's boundaries and outlining what is inside and important to a field and how a field is positioned relative to others (Cramblett Alvarez et al. 2020; Fineman and Gabriel 1994, Harding 2003). These boundaries are the result of initial decisions made about what to include and exclude, as well as the way the included content is categorized, organized and presented. Over time, as these structures are replicated and absorbed into common knowledge, they become self-perpetuating (Giraud 2018; Kuhn 1970; Vicedo 2012).

Consequently, textbooks play an essential role in codifying and disseminating the foundations and what is important in a subject. Moreover, given that attention to history is scant in Management, where most students and scholars only encounter the history of their field in introductory courses and texts, this is the perspective that most will carry through their professional lives. Textbook histories therefore provide excellent insight into the conventional view of Management's understanding of itself (Jones and Khanna 2006; Payne et al. 2006; Smith 2007; Van Fleet and Wren 2005).

The quotation reproduced at the top of this section is taken from the history chapter in one of the best-selling management textbooks (Samson et al. 2021). It appears towards the end of their second chapter titled *The Evolution of Management Thinking*. It is typical of the way in which textbooks treat the development of Sustainable Management.

The second chapter as the 'history chapter', plays an important role in the trope that has become how most Management textbooks begin. In this format, Chapter 1 is where the object and subject, the practice of management and Management Studies, are defined. This chapter then outlines the development of this object and subject. So, for example, in linking the two, Kinicki et al. (2015: 42), begin their Chapter 2 and introduce the earliest approaches to Management (the 'classical perspective'), as follows: "If the name of the game is to manage work more efficiently, what can the classical viewpoint teach me"? These first two chapters of Management textbooks thereby reinforce one another and the view of the field being introduced to initiates (Cummings et al. 2017).

Their quotation at the head of this section, and Samson et al.'s *Evolution of Management* chapter in general, convey two beliefs that are important here. The first is that Sustainable Management is a new thing, one substantially different from what Management has been about in the past. The second is that Sustainable Management is the latest in a long line of improvements in the field that indicate just how much better, or more evolved, Management is now, compared to when it first became a subject around 100 years ago. Hence, Samson et al. (2021: 60), describe sustainable development as both a "new term" and a "relatively new approach to management", noting that whereas in the past the focus had simply been on achieving "short-term efficiency… leading organizations have [now] left all this behind".

Other best-selling management textbooks portray developments in a similar way.

- In Robbins et al.'s text, titled *Management: The Essentials* (2016: 14–16), sustainable management is the latest in their list of new factors in management grouped under the banner "Reshaping and Redefining Management". It explains that: "What's emerging in the 21st century is the concept of managing for sustainability".
- For Kinicki et al.'s *Management: A Practical Introduction* (2015: 8–12), sustainability is a 'megatrend': a brand new challenge for those who aspire to be 'an exceptional manager' in a world where the 'future will not resemble the past'.
- In Schermehorn et al.'s *Management* (2020: 139–140), sustainable management has been a growing focus in 'recent years' since the release of the United Nations report titled 'Our Common Future' in 1987, to the point where sustainability has become "the buzzword in many organizations since the early 2000s".[2]

As Samson et al. (2021: 58, 60), note at the end of their *Evolution of Management* chapter: "management continues to evolve"; restated two pages later as "the field of management just keeps evolving". This nicely bookends the chapter which began by describing the history that would follow with the diagram in Fig. 2.1.

Tracing these books across their multiple editions, back to their first incarnations in the late 1970s, reveals how new trends have been added on top as Management has evolved, creating new buzzwords and megatrends and growing the mountain of Management knowledge. Systems

[2] It may be worth noting for those unfamiliar with management discourse that terms like Megatrend and Buzzword are not used pejoratively here, they are positive signifiers.

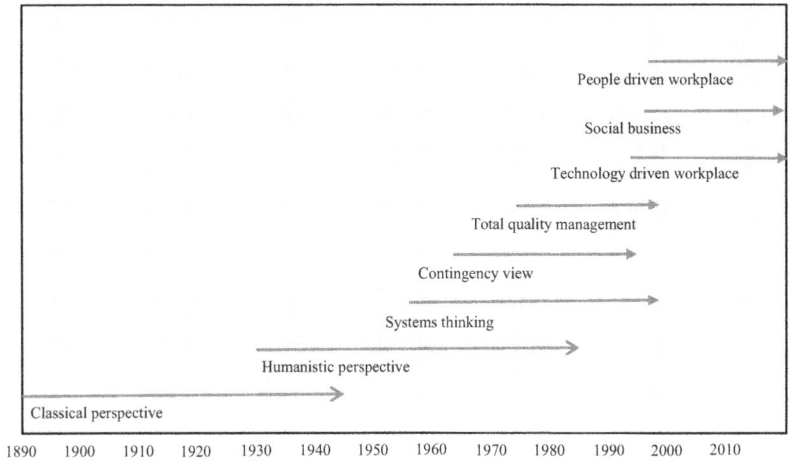

Fig. 2.1 'Management Perspectives Over Time' (Adapted from Samson et al. *Management*, 2021: 40)

Thinking was new once. As was the Contingency Approach, the importance of Culture, Business Ethics, Innovation, and so on. In the edition published in 2000, Total Quality Management and The Learning Organization were at the pinnacle: the 'newest new' things. By 2017, The Technology-Driven Workplace and Open (collaborative) Innovation had been added. In 2021, Social Business and the People-Driven Workplace are the new levels. And Sustainable Management comes after this in Samson et al.'s 2021 *Evolution of Management* chapter. In this, and other Management textbooks, it is both the latest new thing and 'other than', above and beyond what Management has been about before.

Figure 2.1 illustrates how management history is seen to develop, and also provides an organizational schema for the chapter. First, the 'classical perspective' which was developed at the turn of the twentieth century is described. Then the chapter will move through different additional perspectives and schools of thought chronologically to demonstrate a continuous evolution. Then, because it is so new and different, Sustainable Management will appear at the end. At the same time, the thinking embodied in Fig. 2.1 also outlines the distinction made between the subject and the object, with the subject Management falling within the box, while the object, or practice of management, trails back in time prior to it (Tsoukas and Cummings 1997). While the other textbooks mentioned above do not provide a diagram, the same logic is followed, and some less well-known texts provide a similar graphical illustration, For example, Dyck and Neubert's *Management: Current Practices and New Directions* (2008: 30–31), in their column labelled 'The Future', describes a recognition in Management that its "emphasis on maximizing materialist-individualist goals gets in the way of other forms of well-being (e.g., social, ecological)".

In this way, that the object of management can be regarded as much older than the subject Management, enabling 'noble civilizations' to be linked in to provide greater gravitas to the field. So, Samson et al. (2021: 40), can actually begin their history in this way:

> The practice of management can be traced to 3000BCE, to the first government organizations developed by the Sumerians and the Egyptians, but the formal study of management is relatively recent. The early study of management [began with] the classical perspective.

The other textbooks draw the same distinction, but do not pause to explain it. However, Duncan's *Great ideas in management: lessons from the founders and foundations of managerial practice* (1990: 2) provides more detail on why the lines are drawn as they are:

> We certainly could begin in the fourteenth century with Machiavelli [and] no doubt we could learn much from Moses, perhaps Jethro, and maybe even 'old Nick'... Of course there were managers and organizations, and some people understood management processes and leadership. But there was no discipline management. The seeds of management thought were not planted when people started doing management; they were sowed, quite literally, into the soil of human history when people started trying to make sense out of what was being done. Management as a discipline began when people started systematizing it, codifying it, and developing prescriptions for how to manage it better. Eventually, theories that could be taught and learned emerged. That was the beginning of management.

This explains the distinction that Management textbooks make, and why they can see the object of management as *dating back to* ancient civilizations like the Egyptians, Romans and Chinese, who practiced good management (efficiently planning, organizing, directing and controlling things—see Robbins et al. 2016: 25) to build pyramids, aqueducts and great walls; and Management—the subject—*starting* around 1900.

However, not being as pointed about this as Duncan, enables management histories to have their cake and eat it too. Management, these books tell students, is at once 'ancient and noble' like our great predecessors, but evolving and modern and 'better than' previous generations understandings.

Despite these separate origin lines, what binds the object and subject of Management is it's 'good', and it is this, because it is understood to be quite different from the good of Sustainable Management, that marks Sustainable Management out as both new and apart from the Management Studies generally. For whereas other new ideas have simply been added to the production line of improvements, Sustainable Management appears to stand apart, added to and floating over, rather than evolved from: for it serves an end that appears foreign to the subject of Management.

2.2 The Good and the Origin of Management (and How Sustainable Management Does Not Fit)

While we might tend to think that a subject can emerge separately from an object and a determination of what the good of that subject and object is, and that historians record these facts at a later date, Foucault's counter-historical approach encourages us to observe how the good of a subject can be determined and then reversed or stitched back into the fabric of a thing by those who create history. Those who determined what the good of Management was in the middle decades of the twentieth century at the same time invented what the origin of Management that matched this good should be. And both the good and the origin of Management. created in this way, make it seem that Sustainable Management is made from a very different cloth.

2.2.1 The Good of Management

Whether public or private, the basic 'good' is efficiency.

Luther Gulick, in *Papers in the Science of Administration*, Gulick and Urwick Eds. (1937: 191)

So if Sustainable Management is now seen as a new and different way, what defined the old way that it is a break from? And what is it that enables ancient civilizations and thinkers to be added as part of the continuous chain of good management practice, giving the subject extra gravitas, when Sustainable Management is seen as a discontinuity? The answer is the definition of the good of Management.

For the philosopher or the natural scientist the good aspired to is the truth of human experience and the world around us, and getting closer to that truth. The medical doctor could find focus and purpose in looking back to the principles of Hippocrates: first do no harm then apply the hard-won scientific gains of physicians past to advance medical knowledge and protect and preserve the lives of patients. Architects could refer to Vitruvius' *De Architectura* to find that good architecture combines firmatis (durability), utilitas (utility) and venustatis (beauty). But what would we define as the guiding good for management scholars and practitioners, or the key performance indicator that would define their field of endeavour?

The conventional view of the good of management emerged in the first histories or retrospective accounts of Management written up in the 1920s and 30s. A central question the writers of these texts sought to answer as they presented their fledgling subject was: what is Management's end, what is the good that it seeks to advance?

By the 1930s, those who looked back at the development of management as an object of study were clear. As Luther Gulick put it: "efficiency is the fundamental value upon which the science of administration may be erected"; "efficiency [as increasing the ratio of outputs over inputs] is thus axiom number one in the value scale"; and for Management: "whether public or private, the basic 'good' is efficiency" (Gulick and Urwick 1937: 191, 192).

By the middle of the twentieth century, Dwight Waldo (1948: 201) built upon this by drawing a distinction between 'economy' which had earlier been used to define a businessperson's purpose, and 'efficiency', indicating that whereas economy meant spending less, efficiency could mean spending more if the gains made were proportionately greater. Because efficiency could mean spending more or less, it was, claimed Waldo, "true economy": "Efficiency is therefore", he concluded, "the fundamental concept" of management.

This view weaved with the practice of management and the growing professional class of managers. This group was creating a new market for popular books and perhaps the first writer of management 'best-sellers', Peter Drucker (1946: 44), wrote that "The purpose of the corporation [and] 'The Yardstick' [for managers] is to be economically efficient". Other leading scholars and popular writers in this period, such as Chester Barnard, Herbert Simon and Alfred Chandler also saw efficiency as central (Callender 2008).[3]

The first management textbook for tertiary level students brought these views together to conclude that: "The body of management knowledge [focusses on] develop[ing] the most efficient means to organize" (Davis and Filley 1945: 23ff.). Then, after the Second World War, it was decided that the many business schools where management was taught in the United States, which had grown in number and in type since the first decade of the twentieth century, needed to be standardized. And they came to be standardized in a form that reinforced the definition of management's good. Business schools came to be allied to, and Management seen as an extension of, Economics.

After the War, the recently formed American Association of Collegiate Schools of Business (AACSB), started to require that business schools seeking membership must offer instruction in economics, accounting, statistics, business law and finance (McKenna 1989). Further standardization was on the horizon. By the mid-1950s "the science known as economics had often been defined as *the* social science of business" (van Metre 1954: 7, emphasis added). But this assumption was confirmed by two important studies published at the end of the 1950s and sanctioned by the AASCB: Pierson's (1959) *The Education of the American Businessman*, sponsored by the Carnegie Foundation, and Gordon and Howell's (1959) *Higher Education for Business*, sponsored by the Ford Company. The authors of both reports were economists, collaborated closely and their works consequently came to the same conclusions. In particular, that the proper standardization of business schools' curricula must be based on economics (Leontiades 1989).

[3] Barnard spends many words trying to define the difference between effectiveness and efficiency throughout *The Functions of the Executive* (1938). He arrives at an exceedingly esoteric view unlikely to have moved the needle away from relating efficiency to economic efficiency in the mind of managers.

The studies determined the main problem, or in Foucauldian terms the 'problematization': Management was still taught as "a vague, shifting, rather formless subject in which neither the foundations at the undergraduate level nor the super-structure at the graduate level can be sharply defined" (Pierson 1959: 233); and "Dozens of minor fields of specialization have been permitted to develop that never should have been introduced at all" (Gordon and Howell 1959: 217). This was a major reason why business schools were not taken seriously by many major universities, and why management scholars were disregarded by other academics. The Ford and Carnegie studies concluded that "there is a need for a general tightening of standards in terms of the scope of the core studies" (Pierson 1959: 196).

Pierson (1959) argued that this tightening must be focussed around Economics: "Economics has traditionally provided the only theoretical framework for the study of business, and even today the two fields are so closely related they can hardly be discussed separately". Gordon and Howell's model was organized around three disciplines: behavioural sciences (like Psychology), Applied Mathematics and also, but primarily, Economics. Just a few years after the reports were published, Mosson's comparative history of management education systems (1967: 198, see also McKenna 1989) found their recommendations taking effect: Economics had become 'the dominant discipline' in business schools.

Locke's *Management Education since the 1940s* (1989: 5) outlined the problem that business schools were seeking to overcome and that the subject of economics could solve in the middle of the twentieth century:

> The gap [between management and becoming an accepted university discipline] was hard to fill, for it was not a question of finding an existing bridge between theory and practice, one that had been shrouded in a fog of haughty academic prejudice, but of building a bridge between the two. People who established business schools in institutions of higher education quickly learned this lesson for there was, at the outset, no discipline to teach. Science based management had to be invented.

Economics became the science that provided business schools and management's bridge between being a serious academic subject and continuing to appeal to managers and prospective managers as a practical endeavour. And the timing for inventing this bridge was perfect.

Eighty years earlier, economics itself had yet to become a science to be taken seriously in universities. In the late nineteenth century most economists were of the Institutional school, which drew from Adam Smith's more historical and humanistic interests. Empirical, inductive and non-theoretical in orientation, this school encouraged research into specific socio-economic contexts. This was not the stuff to gain acceptance from the mainstream scholarship of the day. Historical-Institutional economics was not a traditional art, nor did it replicate the form of a modern science.

Forty years prior to the Carnegie and Ford reports, economics had secured its own entry to the halls of academia but in doing so had become too abstract and theoretical to be seen as in any way useful to managers (Bell and Kristol 1981). Subsequently, commentators of the time saw an irredeemable divide between economics and management or 'business economics':

> Economics and business economics [may] handle, to a large extent, the same material but they do not have the same spirit. Economics is a philosophical science with philosophical characteristics. Business economics is, on the other hand, an applied science. Chemistry and mechanical technology are closer in spirit to business economics than is economics. (Schmalenbach 1919)

Relatedly, professors of economics in this period were not interested in crossing the divide. They looked at business schools with distain (Sass 1982; Locke 1989).

However, economists began to embrace the use of modern statistical methods and probabilities rather than abstract theories in the middle decades of the twentieth century. These approaches were grounded in science and potentially useful to managers (Cummings 2002). In the mid-1950s, van Metre (1954: 7) described this 'evolution of economics' as follows:

> A highly interesting and unforeseen development which has paralleled the growth of business education in American universities has been the transformation in the science known as economics... Economists are today treading the paths of science in search of signposts to economic truths, rather than scanning the skies of speculative thought for guides to the interpretation of social action. Business practitioners, business teachers and economic scientists all work in varying degrees with the same data in devising their respective plans and procedures. It is important that the

> body of such data be adequate and that it undergo interpretation relevant to necessary uses in business practice, business education and in the shaping of public policies. Schools of business form the best available middle ground for a juncture of forces pursuing these objectives by businessmen and economists.

As business schools became a more accepted part of the academic world by aligning with Economics, the growth in the number of degrees they conferred continued to increase, and through the 1960s and 70s the focus on efficiency as *the* good or end of Management and a manager's endeavours was redoubled. Harold Koontz, for example, was adamant that 'increasing efficiency' was both the 'goal of all managers' and the purpose for developing theory (Koontz and O'Donnell 1974: 7; Koontz 1961). While recent times have seen a shift in terminology, different expressions such as performance, productivity and return on investment are all applied as measures of financial outputs over inputs (Shenhav et al. 1995: 753; see also Lubatkin and Shrieves 1986).

Indeed, the assumption that this is what Management fundamentally aims to advance has deepened, to the extent that even when a critique of economic efficiency as it's good is widely cited, it is misconstrued. For example, responses to March and Sutton's (1997) fundamental argument against economic efficiency suggests the answer is to develop better approaches to measuring it (Richard et al. 2009: 719, 721; see also Durand and Vaara 2009). And while developments post the 1990s have encouraged some to emphasize alternative environmental and social measures of performance, in most managers and researchers' minds these are still secondary, at best, to economic efficiency measures (Hahn and Figge 2011; Maurer et al. 2011). In short, greater financial or economic efficiency remains, 'the primary outcome of interest' for Management (Dass and Shropshire 2012: 702).

But the good of economic efficiency is not the primary outcome of interest for Sustainable Management. This is why it appears to be something both new to and other than Management as we know it. In addition, the conventional history of Management, which folds in and reinforces the understanding of the good of the field, promotes an origin story that seems completely different than where Sustainable Management comes from.

2.2.2 The Origin of Management

If you had to pinpoint the year that modern management theory was born, 1911 might be a logical choice. This was the year Frederick Winslow Taylor's Principles of Scientific Management *was published.*

Robbins et al. *Management* (2015: 46)

Any management textbook or history of management will tell you that the subject's primary founder is Frederick Winslow Taylor. Taylor is the inventor of Scientific Management, an approach for enabling managers to achieve management's universal good: greater efficiency. Thus, it is the subject's first set of relevant theories and the beginning of Management's 'classical perspective'.

Taylor's *Principles of Scientific Management* (1911), where these ideas are first recorded, is consequently seen as a founding document, the field's first book. Often picked out from this testament, by way of illustration, is the now-famous story or case study of how Taylor instructed a labourer called Schmidt to change his habits to become more efficient, enabling him to earn more and the company to be more profitable (Wrege and Perroni 1974).

Given our interest here in highlighting conventional discontinuities and continuities, Taylor's invention is regarded as an important break, but it is also seen as a continuation of a deeper heritage: the approaches of the industrial barons of the nineteenth and early twentieth century; the advances made by industrial engineers; Adam Smith's "ideas of efficient production through specialized labor" (Schermerhorn et al. 2020: 37); and 'noble' civilizations of the past (e.g., the Sumerians, the Chinese, the Romans, etc.—Schermerhorn et al. 2020: 37; Samson et al. 2021: 40). These examples show that the quest for the good of efficiency continues back into ancient times (Tsoukas and Cummings 1997). Adding these deep historical roots supports the rightness of present conventions. "The Egyptian pyramids and the Great Wall of China, for instance, are proof... [that] organized endeavours directed by people responsible for planning, organizing, leading and controlling activities have existed for thousands of years" (Robbins et al. 2016: 44).

Despite these deeper connections, Taylor marks the breakthrough between management merely being practiced, and Management being a proper subject. Taylor's work was the first to recognize and promote the "gospel of efficiency" and Management to the world (Wren 1972: 147). Subsequently, "Frederick Winslow Taylor [is] the origin" because he "recognized that there is a general ability to manage which can be made the subject of a recognized 'discipline'" (Light 1966: 10, 17). Hence, "any book which attempts to show how management thought was developed must inevitably start with Fredrick Winslow Taylor" (Pollard 1974: 3; see also Kelly 1968; Brech, 1967).

In summary, before Taylor Management was not a subject. After him it was. In this way, Taylor becomes to Management what Adam Smith is to Economics: its father. This is one of the first facts taught in many Management 101 classes.

Management histories explain Taylor's rise as the continuation of a growing interest in using emerging technology to alleviate conditions that were highlighting the need for greater efficiency and developed hand-in-hand with advances in large business organizations. Industrialization was increasing, but production methods were crude and with labour in short supply, there was a need to improve productivity (Kinicki et al. 2015). Workers were producing less than they were capable of because of inefficient work methods (Schermerhorn et al. 2020). The Industrial Revolution had enhanced the popularity of the division of labor, but there was still a need to maximize efficiency (Robbins et al. 2016). Management decisions were unsystematic and production efficiency was poor (Bateman and Snell 2009). These conditions led to the emergence of what Samson et al. (2021: 40), call "a new sub-species of economic man – the salaried manager". Taylor's principles provide this new subspecies with the first useful theories with which to achieve their goal—increased economic efficiency—and are often combined with Henry Ford's famous industrial production line innovations to make a theoretical and empirical pair.

When did this historical perspective of Management emerge? While Taylor was identified as a primary point of origin, the 'father of management' as early as the 1920s (Hapgood 1920: 221), the first widely read management historian, Lyndall Urwick, started publishing his histories in the late 1920s, and Urwick regarded Taylor as the first man of Management, comparing him to "Galileo" (Urwick and Brech 1945: 11). The effort to legitimize Management as a university subject, described above, also inspired a new generation of historians working in the middle decades of the twentieth century to create more scholarly histories that marked

Management out as an important field. These writers: George, Chandler, Wren, Pollard; from which modern Management textbooks take their historical cues, followed Urwick in promoting Taylor as the primary figure (Wren and Hay 1977; Cummings et al. 2017). And the contents of Management and Economic history's academic journals, often cited as further evidence by textbook writers, share a similar set of focal points: industrialization, the division of labour, the focus on efficiency gains and Taylor as the leader of the 'classical' school of Management (Cummings and Bridgman 2016).

From Tayloristic origins then, Management histories lay out their evolutionary narrative. This is apparent in the sequencing of chapters in textbooks: from the simplest/oldest theories to chapters containing more advanced humanistic and organic material. As Schermerhorn et al. (2020: 30) put it "Since [Taylor's time] the science and practices of management have been on a rapid and continuous path of development". This continuous evolution currently culminates in the discovery of the importance of new perspectives such as Sustainable Management: revelations regarded as beyond the imagination of the likes of F.W. Taylor and his contemporaries who would have been dumbfounded by the sustainable practices of today's leading human-centred companies like Google.

Management's conventional historical narrative became that economic efficiency (understood as a ratio that seeks to maximize margins between the value of the product or service and the economic cost of production) has been a key good for all civilized societies. Taylor's work marks a discontinuity by being the first to create a subject to study this object intensely. He then is the origin point of Management and the reference point that subsequent schools of thought build upon. Humanistic perspectives argue that doing more to satisfy human needs can lead to greater efficiency; systems thinking argues that seeing organizations and their environments as systems will enable managers to achieve greater efficiency; and so on, as management thinking evolves.

Hence, Management's historical understanding of its origin story reinforces the convention that the fundamental aim of Management, the universal problem it was developed to solve, the good that it seeks to advance, and the foundation upon which later ideas build upon, is economic efficiency. Because this is different from what Sustainable Management is about, Sustainable Management is understood to come from a different place with a different history.

2.3 Sustainable Management: Child of the 60s, Adopted by Management in the 2000s

Primarily, a focus on sustainability, or Sustainable Management, is regarded as a break, or discontinuity, from Management, a subject that understands its fundamental purpose to be economic efficiency. Textbooks, as we have shown, subsequently present Sustainable Management as other than earlier forms of Management, and as a new way of mitigating its undesirable effects: "Managing for sustainability involves ways to measure, evaluate, compare and monitor the impact of an organization's activities" (Robbins et al. 2015: 369). Its arrival is generally linked to the development of a tool for accounting for Sustainable Management: the Triple Bottom Line. This is often showed diagrammatically as three columns (Fig. 2.2) in a manner similar to the convention in Management textbooks that organizes material around simple frameworks and tools for managers (Bridgman et al. 2019).

This presentation of the Triple Bottom Line generally appears alongside a description of a lineage that includes: the publication of the United Nation's report, often referred to as the Brundtland Report, entitled Our Common Future (this defined sustainability as "the use of current resources to enable society to satisfy current needs without compromising the ability of future generations to meet their needs"—Schermerhorn et al. 2020: 140, quoting the World Commission on Environment and Development from 1987); and the Second Earth Summit held in Rio de Janeiro in 1992. This Earth Summit promoted the view that Sustainable Management had three pillars: economic, social and environmental that needed to be considered by business and public organizations, and this informed the development of Triple Bottom Line accounting.

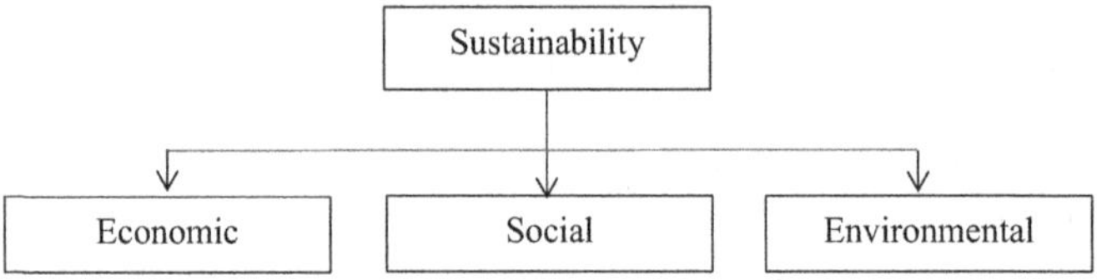

Fig. 2.2 Three Pillars of Sustainable Development (Adapted from Schermerhorn, *Management*, 2020: 140)

The phrase Triple Bottom Line was coined by John Elkington in the 1997 book *Cannibals with Forks*. The title is an adaptation of a question posed by the Polish poet Stanislaw Lec ("Is it progress if a cannibal uses a fork"?), and the phrase reflected another Elkington developed a few years earlier: 'people, planet, profit'. Some claim, however, that these three elements were first articulated by Freer Spreckley in 1981 in a work called *Social Audit—A Management Tool for Co-operative Working*. This argued that enterprises should measure and report on financial performance, social wealth creation and environmental responsibility.

In any event, Elkington's phrase, People, Planet, Profit was adopted as the title of Shell's first 'sustainability report' in 1997, a report that influenced many other organizations and management practice. But profit, planet and people came to be interchangeable with economic (or financial), environmental and social categories in the implementation of Triple Bottom Line reporting, where firms presented their results in terms of environmental and social impact after presenting the conventional economic efficiency measures. Because the practice became to report on social and environmental measures in addition to economic goods, when the TBL is presented in textbooks Economics is usually the first pillar.

Few citations are provided in Management textbooks to support this understanding. Perhaps because it is such a new phenomenon, Robbins et al. (2015: 369) cite the Wikipedia page on Sustainable Management. Here the timeline of the emergence of the new subfield charts its progress in a manner that describes the arrival of this foreign body into the mainstream of Management in five evolutionary phases:

1. *Industrial environmentalism* (1960–1970): Concerns about the environment are acknowledged in some industries, but environmentalists were not viewed as credible sources of information. Industries and business interests were able to resist pressures and create their own definitions and regulations.
2. *Regulatory environmentalism* (1970–1982): The EPA (the United States Environmental Protection Agency) was created in 1970 and became a mediator between environmentalists and industry. During this period, sustainability for managers was only important in terms of compliance with law. It was considered at best a necessary evil and at worst a temporary nuisance, and most companies treated environmental management as a threat, and pollution control expenditures as non-recoverable investments.

3. *Environmentalism as social responsibility* (1982–1988): Activism became more influential, and there was an increase in the funding and memberships of major non-governmental organizations (NGOs). Industries gradually became more cooperative with regulators and new structures were implemented to manage compliance.
4. *Strategic environmentalism* (1988–1993): Some businesses developed a proactive stance on environmental protection. Although this signalled some advancement, the concern for sustainability still kept being pushed down the hierarchy of important things to do.
5. *Environmental management as an opportunity* (1993–present): In this phase, environmental protection comes to be seen not as a threat to business but rather an opportunity, one that could increase competitive advantage in the marketplace, and it becomes increasingly apparent that sustainable management is an emerging norm.

While these textbooks and websites outlining the arrival and development of Sustainable Management from marginal nuisance to buzzword, do not cite an extensive literature, the progress they chart reflects the popular press, commonly held views of practitioners, and the few highly cited scholarly works written on the history of Sustainable Management. For example, Wikipedia's 'five phases' are a carbon copy of those presented in Hoffman's, *From Heresy to Dogma: An Institutional History of Corporate Environmentalism* (2001), probably the most widely cited academic treatise on the topic.

Hoffman and other academics who have written on the history of Sustainable Management or sustainable development (e.g., Du Pisani 2006; Mebratu 1998) also utilize a device that management historians used half a century earlier. They claim that while sustainable management as a thing, or an object, or a problem, predates modernity, it is only in recent times that it has properly become a subject:

> Although corporate environmental problems can be traced back to the industrial revolution and beyond, clear identification of these problems and the development of institutional solutions to them began only in the mid to late 1960s. (Hoffman 2001: 10)

In this way, Sustainable Management—as was the pattern with Management—is at once old (i.e., universally important) and new (i.e., innovative and to be taken seriously now).

Consequently, the common knowledge informed by these sources is that Sustainable Management is a nascent subject with shallow theoretical roots, traceable to the 1970s or 1980s, with perhaps some precursors appearing in the 1960s (e.g., often later developments like the EPA are seen as "the extended shadow of Rachel Carson", whose book about the impact of synthetic parasites, *Silent Spring*, was published in 1962—Henrickson 1991: 84).

Given this perspective, it should be no surprise that popular predictors about the future of management in the 1970s and 80s, works like *The Shock of the New* or *Megatrends*, should make no mention of environmental concerns or sustainable management (Toffler 1970; Naisbett 1982), and that just a couple of decades later it can be seen as a new buzzword, or identified by recently published textbooks as unprecedented megatrends, or that Naomi Klein (2015) can describe the crisis caused as capitalism and conservation clash as unprecedented. Just a few decades ago, before the realization that Sustainable Management was important, people would never have thought of adding it to the manager's toolkit.

2.4 Second Thoughts

Despite it appearing to be early days for Sustainable Management, many are already disappointed with its impact. Almost as soon as some corporate early adopters started recognizing the value of being seen to promote environmental and social goods, critics have cried 'greenwashing'. Madison Avenue advertising executive, Jerry Mander, claimed that firms were subverting the boundaries of environmentalism and misleading the public to increase their profits. Mander (1972) called the way some companies presented themselves as overtly ecologically friendly as 'eco-pornography'. The word 'greenwashing' was created shortly afterwards to name how firms would continue to focus on *the* bottom line: the first and fundamental bottom line of economics, while showing themselves in a positive environmental light through some 'window-dressing' (Kangun et al. 1991).

John Elkington (2018), inventor of the Triple Bottom Line (TBL), has gone further. "How often are management concepts subjected to recalls by the people who invented them? It is hard to think of a single case", Elkington wondered. In an article titled "25 Years Ago I Coined the Phrase 'Triple Bottom Line' Here's Why It's Time to Rethink It", he calls for a 'product recall' on TBL and its application.

Elkington argued that his original idea was to encourage businesses to manage the wider economic, social and environmental impacts of their operations, but its practical use as an accounting tool, whereby firms look first at the financial bottom line (he notes how the economic bottom line has now morphed into financial), and then, secondarily, glance at the other two, has now undermined its value. Despite textbook authors like Samson et al. (2021: 60) thinking that firms would leave their traditional focus on 'short-term economic efficiency' behind them, Elkington seems to be having second thoughts. Seeing the environment and social goods as add-ons, rather than primary elements, may have diluted the framework's intentions: "TBL's stated goal from the outset was *system change* — pushing toward the transformation of capitalism. It was never supposed to be just an accounting system" (Elkington 2018).

∞

This chapter has outlined how Sustainable Management is positioned as, and understood to be, the newest new thing in Management. Its first stirrings emerged in the 1960s and 70s—an age that saw the rise of environmentalism, 'hippy-culture', and what came to be called, sometimes pejoratively, 'new-ageism'. It was then adopted as an additional way to think about Management in recent decades. Sustainable Management's conception marks a discontinuity, something different from how Management has been thought of before.

Our historical understanding has framed our view of the subject and object of management as being defined by its fundamental good: economic efficiency or improving the ratio of economic outputs over economic inputs. While this is an object that has motivated civilizations for millennia, it was only at the beginning of the twentieth century that serious thought and theory development marked out Management as a subject. Sustainable Management is seen to be different. It seeks to add new aims related to the conservation of the environment and social justice and well-being to the manager's mindset. But while gains have been made, Sustainable Management has faced an uphill battle to overcome the fundamental primacy of economic efficiency.

Echoing the conventional history represented in this chapter, Lubin and Etsy (2010), also describe Sustainable Management as a new 'megatrend': the latest new thing for managers to become cognizant of in a line of "incipient societal and economic shifts such as globalization, the rise of the information society, and the move from hierarchical organizations to networks". They outline a model with which managers can handle sustainability, with four phases of value creation focused on doing things completely anew: *Transforming* core business; Developing *new* business model creation and differentiation; Doing new things in *new* ways and Doing old things in *new* ways.

Effecting meaningful change by forgetting the past and grasping the new makes sense. But the counter-history in the next chapter may cause us to question this. It leads us to see that we might progress Sustainable Management more effectively by encouraging people to focus less on the new, and more on some very old ways. Because maybe Sustainable Management would be less easy to work around, see superficially, and treat as a new trend waiting to be surpassed by the next one, if it was not seen as such an 'add-on'.

What if another history helped us to recognize other points of origin? Helped us to see that sustainability could have been both at the heart of those who created Management over 100 years ago, and the very good they believed it would serve? This second history could help us address the second thoughts expressed by Elkington and others.

References

Barnard, C. 1938. *The functions of the executive*. Cambridge: Harvard University Press.

Bateman, T.S., and S.S. Snell. 2009. *Management: Leading & collaborating in a competitive world*, 8th ed. Boston: McGraw-Hill.

Bell, D., and I. Kristol. 1981. *The crisis in economic theory*. New York: Basic Books.

Bridgman, T., S. Cummings, and J. Ballard. 2019. Who built Maslow's pyramid? A history of the creation of management studies' most famous symbol and its implications for management education. *Academy of Management Learning & Education* 18 (1): 81–98.

Callender, G. 2008. *Efficiency and management*. London: Routledge.

Cramblett Alvarez, L.D.C., J.L. Leach, J.L. Rodriguez, and N. Jones. 2020. Unsung psychology pioneers: A content analysis of who makes history (and who doesn't). *American Journal of Psychology* 133 (2): 241–262.

Cummings, S. 2002. *Recreating strategy*. London: Sage.

Cummings, S., and T. Bridgman. 2016. The Limits and possibilities of history: How a wider, deeper and more engaged understanding of business history can foster innovative thinking. *Academy of Management Learning and Education* 15 (2): 1–18.

Cummings, S., T. Bridgman, J. Hassard, and M. Rowlinson. 2017. *A new history of management*. Cambridge: Cambridge University Press.

Dass, M., and C. Shropshire. 2012. Introducing functional data analysis to managerial science. *Organizational Research Methods* 15 (4): 693–721.
Davis, R.C., and A.C. Filley. 1945. *Principles of management*. New York: Alexander Hamilton Institute.
Deleuze, G. 1988. *Foucault*. Minneapolis: University of Minnesota Press.
Drucker, P.F. 1946/1964. *The concept of the corporation*. New York: Mentor.
Duncan, W.J. 1990. *Great ideas in management—Lessons from the founders and foundations of managerial practice*. San Francisco, CA: Jossey-Bass.
Du Pisani, J.A. 2006. Sustainable development—Historical roots of the concept. *Environmental Sciences* 3 (2): 83–96.
Durand, R., and E. Vaara. 2009. Causation, counterfactuals and competitive advantage. *Strategic Management Journal* 30: 1245–1264.
Elkington, J. 2018. *25 years ago I coined the phrase 'Triple Bottom Line' Here's why it's time to rethink it*. HBR Online. https://hbr.org/2018/06/25-years-ago-i-coined-the-phrase-triple-bottom-line-heres-why-im-giving-up-on-it.
Fineman, S., and Y. Gabriel. 1994. Paradigms of organizations: An exploration in textbook rhetorics. *Organization* 1 (2): 375–399.
Foucault, M. 1988. An interview with Michel Foucault conducted by Michael Bess, San Francisco. *History of the present* 4 (Spring 1988): 1–13.
Giraud, Y. 2018. Textbooks in the history of recent economics: The case of Samuelson's Economics. *History of political economy* 50 (3): 579–585.
Gordon, R., and J. Howell. 1959. *Higher education for business*. New York: Columbia University Press.
Gulick, L.H., and Urwick, L.F. (eds.). 1937. *Papers in the science of administration*. New York: Columbia University Press.
Hahn, T., and F. Figge. 2011. Beyond the bounded instrumentality in current corporate sustainability research: Toward an inclusive notion of profitability. *Journal of Business Ethics* 104: 325–345.
Hapgood, N. 1920. *The advancing hour*. New York: Boni & Liveright.
Harding, N. 2003. *The social construction of management: Texts and identities*. London: Routledge.
Henricksson, J. 1991. *Rachel Carson: The environmental movement*. Millbrook Press.
Hoffman, A.J. 2001. *From heresy to dogma: An institutional history of corporate environmentalism*. Stanford: Stanford University Press.
Jones, G., and T. Khanna. 2006. Bringing history (back) into international business. *Journal of International Business Studies* 37: 453–468.
Kangun, N., L. Carlson, and S.J. Grove. 1991. Environmental advertising claims: A preliminary investigation. *Journal of Public Policy & Marketing* 10 (2): 47–58.
Kelly, J. 1968. *Is scientific management possible?*. London: Faber & Faber.
Kinicki, A., B.D., Scott-Ladd, M. Perry, and B. Williams. 2015. *Management: A practical introduction*. Sydney: McGraw Hill Australia.

Klein, N. 2015. *This changes everything: Capitalism versus the climate*. New York: Simon & Schuster.
Koontz, H. 1961. The management theory jungle. *Academy of Management Journal* 4: 174–188.
Koontz, H., and C. O'Donnell. 1974. *Essentials of management*. New York: McGraw-Hill.
Kuhn, T.S. 1970. *The structure of scientific revolutions*, 2nd ed. Chicago: University of Chicago Press.
Leontiades, M. 1989. *Myth management: An examination of corporate diversification as fact and theory*. Oxford: Blackwell.
Light, H.R. 1966. *The nature of management*. London: Pitman.
Locke, R. 1989. *Management and education since 1940: The influence of America and Japan on West Germany, Great Britain, and France*. Cambridge: Cambridge University Press.
Lubatkin, M., and R.E. Shrieves. 1986. Toward reconciliation of market performance measures to strategic management research. *Academy of Management Review* 11 (3): 497–512.
Lubin, D.A., and D.C. Esty. 2010. The sustainability imperative. *Harvard Business Review* 88 (5): 42–50.
Mander, J. 1972. Ecopornography: One year and nearly a billion dollars later. *Advertising Owns Ecology, Communication and Arts Magazine* 14 (2): 45–56.
March, J., and R.I. Sutton. 1997. Organizational performance as a dependent variable. *Organization Science* 8 (6): 698–706.
Maurer, C.C., P. Bansal, and M.M. Crossan. 2011. Creating economic value through social values: Introducing a culturally informed resource-based view. *Organization Science* 22 (2): 432–448.
McKenna, J. F. 1989. Management education in the United States. In *Management education: An international survey*, ed. W. Bryt, 18–54. London: Routledge.
Mebratu, D. 1998. Sustainability and sustainable development: Historical and conceptual review. *Environmental Impact Assessment Review* 18 (6): 493–520.
Mosson, T. 1967. Introduction. In *Teaching the process of management: The proceedings of an international seminar*. London: Harrap.
Naisbett, J. 1982. *Megatrends*. New York: Warner.
Payne, S.C., S.S. Youngcourt, K.M. Watrous. 2006. Portrayals of F.W. Taylor across textbooks. *Journal of Management History* 12 (4): 385–407.
Pierson, F. 1959. *The education of American businessmen: A study of university-collegiate programs in business education*. New York: McGraw-Hill.
Pollard, H.R. 1974. *Developments in management thought*. London: Heinemann.
Richard, P.J., T.M. Devinney, G.S. Yip, and G. Johnson. 2009. Measuring organizational performance: Towards methodological best practice. *Journal of Management* 35: 718–804.
Robbins, S., P. Bergman, I. Stagg, M. Coulter. 2015. *Management*, 7th ed. Frenchs Forest: Pearson Australia.

Robbins, S., D. DeCenzo, M. Coulter, M. Woods. 2016. *Management: The Essentials*, 3rd ed. Pearson Australia.

Samson, D., T. Donnet, and R.L. Daft. 2021. *Management*, 7th ed. Melbourne: Cengage Australia.

Sass, S.A. 1982. *The pragmatic imagination: A history of the Wharton School, 1881–1981.* Philadelphia, PA: Wharton.

Schermerhorn, J.R., P. Davidson, D. Poole, P. Woods, A. Simon, E. McBarron, F. Junaid. 2020. *Management*. Milton: Wiley Australia.

Schmalenbach, E. 1919. Selbstkostenrechnung. *ZfhF* 13: 257–299.

Shenhav, Y. 1995. From chaos to systems: The engineering foundations of organization theory, 1879–1932. *Administrative Science Quarterly*, 40: 557–585.

Smith, G.E. 2007. Management history and historical context: Potential benefits of its inclusion in the management curriculum. *Academy of Management Learning & Education* 6: 522–533.

Stambaugh, J.E., and C.Q. Trank. 2010. Not so simple: Integrating new research into textbooks. *Academy of Management Learning & Education* 9: 663–681.

Taylor, F.W. 1911. *The principles of scientific management*. New York: Harper & Row.

Toffler, A. 1970. *Future shock*. London: Pan

Tsoukas, H., and S. Cummings. 1997. Marginalization and recovery: The emergence of Aristotelian themes in organization studies. *Organization Studies* 18 (4): 655–683.

Urwick, L.F., and E.F.L. Brech. 1945. *The making of scientific management—Volume 1: Thirteen pioneers*. London: Pitman.

Van Fleet, D.D., and D.A. Wren. 2005. Teaching history in business schools: 1982-2003. *Academy of Management Learning & Education* 4 (1): 44–56.

van Merte, T.W. 1954. *A history of the Graduate School of Business, Columbia University*. New York: Columbia University Press.

Vicedo, M. 2012. Introduction: The secret lives of textbooks. *Isis* 103 (1): 83–87.

Waldo, D. 1948. *The administrative state*. New York: Roland.

Wrege, C., and A. Perroni. 1974. Taylor's pig tale: A historical analysis of Frederick W. Taylor's pig-iron experiments. *Academy of Management Journal* 17: 6–27.

Wren, D.A. 1972/1994. *The evolution of management thought* (1st/4th editions). Ronald Press: New York.

Wren, D.A., and R.D. Hay. 1977. Management historians and business historians: Differing perceptions of pioneer contributors. *Academy of Management Journal* 20 (3): 470–476.

CHAPTER 3

A Counter-History of Sustainable Management (or How the American Most Hated by Big Business Invented Management)

Abstract Management's conventional historical narrative is that 'the father' of Management is F.W. Taylor. While efficiency has been a universal concern of all great civilizations, Taylor was the first to preach the 'gospel of efficiency' and develop theories that enabled managers to achieve it. This origin story reinforces the belief that the good that defines Management is economic efficiency. However, the counter-history developed in this chapter looks at the period prior to Taylor's publication of the book seen as Management's first document in 1911, to investigate where the approach attributed to Taylor—Scientific Management—came from. We unearth a forgotten founder with a very different view. Louis Brandeis developed Scientific Management in 1910. It was shaped by his professional practice over three decades and Brandeis defined its good or motive as conservation: or what we today might term sustainability.

Keywords Frederick Taylor · Louis Brandeis · Conservation · Sustainability · Economic Efficiency · Social Goods

Histories inform us that Management's point of origin is Frederick Winslow Taylor. He is the first person to fully apply himself to understand the object of management, and to develop a body of theory to advance

S. Cummings and T. Bridgman, *The Past, Present and Future of Sustainable Management*,
https://doi.org/10.1007/978-3-030-71076-7_3

its universal good of economic efficiency. Some great civilizations, and a few other great men (like Adam Smith who had recognized the importance of efficiency in combination with *laissez-faire* economics), may be seen as forebears and indicative of management and efficiency as continuous universal concerns, but Taylor was the first to explicitly recognize the need to create Management as a subject. Taylor's timing was good. His foundation of Management dovetailed with and was designed to *advance* continuing industrialization and the growth of big business in America and in other developed countries.

Taylor is, therefore, fundamental to Management. But he was flawed and his ideas simplistic, so history shows us how the field continuously evolves from his origins, as the best sciences do, improving upon his foundations by adding new and better approaches. The latest significant addition to Management's cannon is sustainability. Sustainable Management stands then as a historical discontinuity: a new imperative that only we today are clever enough to recognize the importance of. It is an imperative that could not have been conceived in earlier times in the less developed minds of the subject's founders.

This chapter chips away at these conventional views of history. Informed by the approaches of Michel Foucault, its counter-history aims to disrupt conventional understandings of Management's development: in particular the notion of Taylor as the field's founder and the related understanding of his work as the point of origin that helps define the subject and object.

Beginning with a juxtaposition of quotations, we unpick the idea that economic efficiency has been a continuous aim for all humankind, and that its management was a driving force for all great civilizations. On the contrary, we suggest that its sudden emergence marks instead a particular discontinuity; and it shows how the intellectual ferment that led to the establishment of Management can be understood to be driven by other problematizations, not by an objective uncovering or realization of the importance of efficiency.

Our counter-history puts forward an alternative: that Management was developed to showcase a new way of managing a business during a legal case. But the ideas that informed its creation and the view of good management it promoted emerged in response to a broader problematization. This was how to create an alternative ideology *in opposition to* laissez-faire industrialization and big business running rampant. This ideology was 'conservation' and it was a movement for sustainability.

Consequently, this counter-history will show that Sustainable Management was not just at the forefront of the minds of those who first made Management: more than this, it was regarded as Management's fundamental good.

In so doing, this chapter critiques the idea that Management began with Frederick Taylor. It argues, to paraphrase Foucault, that if we seek to free thought from what it silent thinks about Management, and think differently, lawyer Louis Brandeis, could be considered the key founder of the field. And, it offers a critique of the belief that economic efficiency is management's fundamental good. Economic efficiency is rather a particular object that was brought to the fore as later thinkers sought to define Management in response to a different problem: legitimating Management as a profession and an academic subject in the middle of the twentieth century. Subsequently, it was economic efficiency that became Management's defining fundamental good and Taylor the subject's founder, after the fact, and as Brandeis faded from view.

This counter-history consequently seeks to dig up another genealogy, and turn the history of Sustainable Management on its head. It suggests that sustainability is not a new thing in Management. It suggests instead that sustainability can be seen as a very old element. And it argues that rather than an addition, the newest new thing in Management, sustainability can be regarded as being at the heart of the enterprise. It was the reason Management was created.

This counter-history will subsequently enable us to create a new, and quite different history of Sustainable Management in the next chapter, one that reverses many conventional continuities and assumed innovations. But we begin this chapter with a device that Foucault (e.g., Foucault 1970, 1977a) is often noted for: a juxtaposition of texts that highlights a largely unrecognized discontinuity: a world in which a particular understanding of efficiency is not a general good, and, just a few years later, one in which it is.

3.1 Efficiency Made Good

The two quotations below are translations of the same passage from Aristotle's *Metaphysics* (italics added). The first is from Smith and Ross' Oxford translation of 1908. The second is from the first page of *The Functions of the Executive* by Chester Barnard published in 1938: a book described as "the most influential book in the entire field of management since Taylor's *Scientific Management*" (Koontz 1980: 51; cf. George 1972).

> We must consider also in which of the two ways the nature of the universe contains the good or the highest good, whether as something separate and by itself, or as the order of the parts. Probably in both ways, as an army does. *For the good* is found in the order and the leader, and more in the later; for he does not depend on the order but it depends on him.
>
> Aristotle *Metaphysics* (XII, *1075a*).
> Translation, Smith and Ross (Oxford: 1908)

> *For the efficiency* of an army consists partly in the order and partly in the general; but chiefly in the latter, because he does not depend upon the order, but the order depends upon him.
>
> Aristotle *Metaphysics* (XII, *1075a*). In Barnard (1938).
> Translation, Tredennick (Cambridge, MA: 1935)

The translation Barnard uses is Tredennick's Harvard University Press edition developed in the late 1920s. This quotation, with which his *Functions of the Executive* begins, is thus cast with the authority of Aristotle, serving to show how important leadership is and the desired end towards which management leadership is set: efficiency. But what strikes the reader upon the juxtaposition of the two quotations above is the lack of the word efficiency in the 1908 translation. By the 1930s, efficiency has become a synonym of 'the good'. But in 1908, as we will explain, efficiency would have been an unfathomable translation.

Barnard's excerpt starts part way into the passage, turning 'For the efficiency…' into the beginning of a sentence (so we do not see that Aristotle was using relations between a general and an army as an analogy to describe how the world is given form). But whatever the motivation for Barnard's editing of the sentence, the word efficiency is true to Tredennick's translation. Translations of this work prior to Tredennick's, and most afterwards, do not use the word efficiency. So how did efficiency become a key element in Tredennick's translation of Aristotle?

Classical Greek did not have a word to equate with efficiency as we read it now, nor did English until the end of the nineteenth century. The common modern understanding of efficiency springs from the combination of different meanings of the word converging at the end of the nineteenth century. The Oxford English Dictionary (1989: IV: 83ff.) describes three main etymological branches of the meaning of efficiency:

> The first from the Latin *efficiens*, which the OED traces from the 16th century, relates to the "fact of being an operative agent or efficient cause" (e.g., 1628. T. Spencer *Logick* 31: "God is said to be the Efficient Cause of man").
>
> The second branch relates to describing a "Fitness or power to accomplish the purpose intended", likely what we would today call 'effectiveness', which dates from the middle of the 17th century.
>
> The third is a specialist definition relating to mechanics and physics dating from the early-19th century where efficiency becomes an expression of "the total energy expended by a machine". By the mid-19th century, this has developed into a performance measure: "The ratio of useful work performed to the total energy expended or taken in".

By the beginning of the twentieth century, as the machine increasingly became a metaphor for understanding the human world, the third branch joined back up with the second to create our modern twentieth and twenty-first-century meaning (Cummings 2002). The OED suggests this originally related only to specialist fields like engineering and economics (and is thus described as "economic, marginal or technical efficiency"), but it grew a wider compass: this is a fitness to accomplish by being able to do more with the same or less, or improving the ratio of outputs over inputs. This was a useful means to achieve other ends.

Looking at primary sources from the period shows that economic efficiency was not regarded as a general good prior to the early decades of the twentieth century. Tracing the use of efficiency in publications using a tool like Google Ngram, shows its use going from next to nothing in the nineteenth century to an upward inflection point after 1910 and plateauing around 1917.[1] Studies point to over 100 articles advocating efficiency appearing in popular magazines in the United States between 1911 and 1914 (Jordan 2005), and this surge is also revealed in

[1] https://books.google.com›ngrams.

newspaper archives, where efficiency suddenly emerges in thousands of advertisements to describe the goodness (their use value being well in excess of their cost) of all manner of products from razor blades to motor oil to health equipment (see Fig. 3.1).

The particularity of economic efficiency as a proclaimed general good can also be observed in the degree to which its new meaning in the second decade of the twentieth century had to be explained. Theodore Roosevelt does not mean economic efficiency but an older meaning here in an 1895 letter: "A citizen has got to be decent of course. That is the first requisite; but the second, and just as important, is that he shall be efficient, and he can't be efficient unless he is manly" (Yale University Library, Walter Camp Papers, Reel 15). In 1904, Veblen (1904: 39) clarified that this new efficiency might be a primary concern of engineers, but not of managers, who might do well to work "against, as well as for, a new more efficient organization". However, the emerging general meaning,

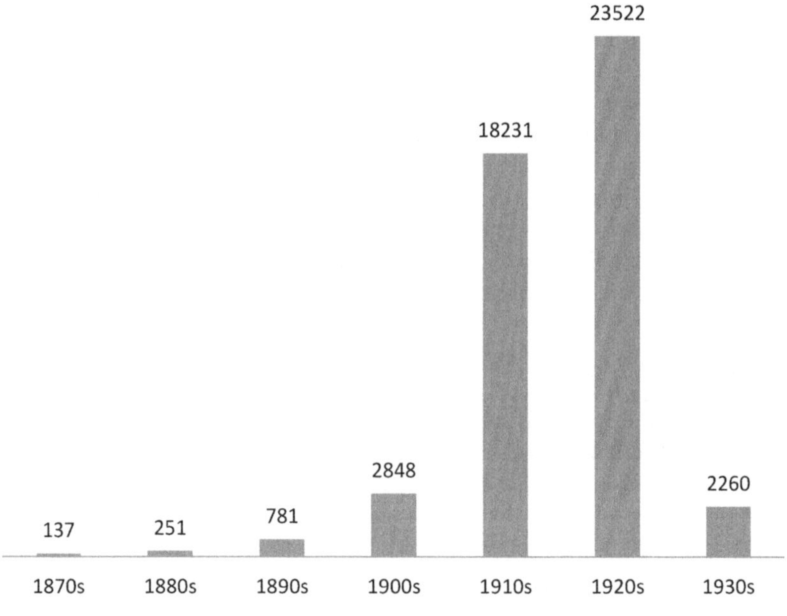

Fig. 3.1 Newspaper advertisements including the word 'efficiency' (Data from the ProQuest Historical Newspapers database)

related to the "energy output-input ratio of a machine" (Haber 1964: ix), would require Casson to explain that: "'Efficiency' ha[s] in the past six or seven years acquired a new and almost technical meaning" (in Gray and Turner 1916: 151); and lead George Seldes (1917) to outline for his British readers how economic efficiency, or what he termed 'American efficiency', was different from their understanding of the term.

After World War I, economic efficiency as a good in its own right took on more significance. Efficiency experts spread out to become important advisors, informing a growing cohort of managers and offering revolutions of a much more mild-mannered nature than the bloody ones happening in Europe. Thus, economic efficiency grew to become a general end that was "reassuringly static and demonstrably effective"; an "All-American Christian virtue", offering a cool and steady rather than a hot-headed energy: a muscular and vital, yet benign, force to lead people beyond troubled times (Jordan 2005: 60ff.; see also Wiebe 1967).

Management history's lens, first developed in the second and third decades of twentieth century (where increasing the margin between output and inputs measured in financial terms was becoming a general performance measure), looked with hindsight and assumed economic efficiency must be a continuous concern through the ages of Man (or at least his noble civilizations). And at the same time, historians picked out Frederick Taylor's work as the subject's point of origin for systematically responding to this concern and embracing a focus on this kind of efficiency when earlier peoples had only partially considered it. Indeed, later in this chapter, the novelty of using the word efficiency as an object in this way in 1910 will be illustrated by the confusion caused by it being inserted into the court case where a new subject, Management, is also introduced for the very first time.

Tredennick may have transposed the original meaning of efficiency into his translation at the beginning of this section, for Aristotle is writing of 'the efficient cause' of things, or effects that God's design caused (Clark 1992). But given that by the 1930s this meaning was "only in philosophical use" (OED 1989: IV: 83), and Tredennick was writing for a general audience, he was far more likely attempting, as translators do, to make Aristotle relatable for contemporary readers. And by the late 1920s, the placement of efficiency as a universal good in Tredennick and Barnard's work appeared natural.

But the sharp decline in the use of efficiency and the reversion of later translations of *Metaphysics* to constructions similar to Smith and

Ross's version of Aristotle rather than Tredennick/Barnard's, suggest that efficiency's status spike was particular and fleeting. While mid-century management histories may have looked back with hindsight to regard economic efficiency as a universal good, social historians note that "efficient and good [only] came close to meaning the same thing" in the early decades of the twentieth century (Haber 1964: ix). They describe its sudden arrival as being like a "flash flood", and compare the fervour surrounding it to a new cult (Haber 1964: 52; Callender 2008). But this specific fervour came to be defined, and is regarded to this day, as the basic or universal good of Management.

While Taylor and his contemporaries were certainly investigating economic efficiency as a means, in 1910 this may not have been the end of their endeavours. But what else could the good that inspired the interest in marginal efficiency and management have been? By trying to think from a perspective prior to and in 1910 rather than after it in hindsight, the following pages in this counter-history will argue that Management's fundamental good was surprisingly similar to what we might consider to be the good of Sustainable Management today. Management's original good was conservation.

3.2 The Formation of Management as a Subject with Conservation at Its Central Motive

RAILROADS COULD SAVE $1,000,000 A DAY.
Brandeis says Scientific Management Would Do it

Front page headline, *New York Times*, November 21, 1910.

The idea that Management was a subject became front-page news on November 21, 1910. It was on this day that Louis Brandeis, representing customers of the Eastern Rail Road Company (ERRC), took an unusual tack in a case before the Interstate Commerce Commission. Brandeis claimed that instead of putting rates up as proposed, the Company could keep them as they were, or even reduce them, and still make more money by applying a new body of knowledge called Scientific Management: a subject that Brandeis himself had formed for the purposes of the case.

The story from the late edition on the 21st was developed further in the early edition on the 22nd of November (p. 6). On the 23rd, the

New York Times gathered together responses to this dramatic claim from a number of dismissive railroad executives and supporters of the ERRC under the headline: "ALL SCOFF AT BRANDEIS. Officials Say Railroads Are Economically Managed" (p. 4). In this way, the rest of the case was framed as a very public fight between old ways of running a corporation and Brandeis's new ways of doing so.

While this hardly seems the stuff of water-cooler conversation, at the time the fight garnered significant public attention. Newspapers were the media in 1910. Almost everyone who could read, read newspapers, and they discussed what they read with one another. American households in this period purchased an average of 3.1 different newspapers a day, a number enabled by the fact that newspapers were extremely cheap (Gordon 2017). *The Times* sold for a penny.

∞

Scientific Management, the term that designated the collection of theories and ideology that mark the first articulation of Management as a subject, was not developed by Frederick W. Taylor in 1911 as we teach students now. It was invented by the man in *The Times* headline: Louis Brandeis.

In 1914, Brandeis was interviewed by Columbia University Ph.D. Candidate, Howard Drury. Drury's dissertation would become the first (but now largely forgotten) history of Management, published as *Scientific Management: A History and Criticism* (Drury 1915). In a letter to Drury, Brandeis wrote that "The term 'scientific management' was not adopted as synonymous with the Taylor system" (Brandeis to Drury, January 31, 1914). So, if it was not this, as later historians and management experts have assumed it to be, what was it, why was it developed and where did it come from?

Brandeis goes on in his letter to explain to Drury what Scientific Management was. The development of Scientific Management was, in his words, a matter of: "expressing the fundamental conception of a new movement... in October 1910 when I was about to bring this movement forward in connection with the rate advance [Eastern Rate] case".

The conception of Scientific Management was important for the Eastern Rate Case because Brandeis's strategy was to argue that the company was being poorly managed; to argue, in other words, that it would not need to put rates up and harm its clients if they applied good management practices. And this new management thinking could be seen as a coherent, if emergent, body of knowledge that the ERRC was negligent for not being cognizant of. Because a movement of one man could not convincingly be construed as a body of knowledge, Brandeis needed others in the fold. To win the case with this strategy, Brandeis explained that (Brandeis to Drury, January 31, 1914):

> It seemed to me important that all differences between the various advocates of efficiency [that had emerged in the last few years] should be eliminated, and some term be adopted to express the new idea which was common to all of them; and I asked all who were to be witnesses to agree on this subject, Several names, like 'Taylor System', 'Functional Management', 'Shop Management', and 'Efficiency', were proposed. It seemed to me that the only term which would properly describe the movement and appeal to the imagination, was 'Scientific Management', and as I recall it all present were ultimately unanimous in the adoption of that term. It was agreed that in presenting the matter to the Interstate Commerce Commission, the fundamental conception, rather than a particular system, should be presented.

'Appealing to the imagination' was Brandeis forte. He was known as 'the people's lawyer' for representing the side of 'the people' against big business or big government and for his ability to harness public opinion. His decision that the amount of money Scientific Management could save the ERRC should be an eye-popping $1,000,000, was designed to elevate the case onto the front pages of the newspapers and before the eyes of the maximum number of citizens.

So if this explains what Scientific Management was and why it was developed at the time it was created, what remains to explore is where it came from: what was 'the movement' that Brandeis saw it as a part of?

In summary, it was a combination of the kind of methods utilized by the consultants Brandeis assembled to be expert witnesses against the ERRC, partly a reflection of Frederick Taylor's ideas as it was these that seemed to connect the ideas of those many and varied consultants. But it was also a response to two problems: the first is the micro one described above—how to show that a company like the ERRC was poorly run for the benefit of the clients that Brandeis was representing; the second was a macro problem—the problem of the conversation of resources as a time where the excesses of laissez-faire industrialization were biting in America. This second problem had led to the rise of the 'conservation movement'. And all of these things were marshalled by Brandeis through the lens of his view of good management practice and the methods for achieving this. Brandeis's understanding of what this was, grew out of his 30 years of experience as a public prosecutor of bad business and a consultant to hundreds of clients on good management.

In the paragraphs below, we will explore the links from the emergence of the conservation movement, to the social concerns that Brandeis saw bad management as exacerbating, through to Brandeis's prosecution of the Eastern Rate Case and back. And later we will explore how Brandeis's view of good management practice was rooted in social and environmental goods and formed in the decades leading up to 1910.

3.2.1 Management for Conservation

Foucault's (1985: 10) work encourages us to see how subjects and objects emerge in response to "the conditions in which human beings' problematize' what they are [and] what they do". The 'problematization' that histories of Management see the field responding to is how to increase productivity as industrialization evolves. The 'problematization' that advocates for, and historians of, Management in the middle of the twentieth century, which encouraged building the bridges with Economics and building standardized business schools, was a search for academic legitimacy. However, running counter to this is a now largely forgotten problematization that promoted the emergence of Management and efficiency as an object and means to achieving Management's ends prior to what we assume Management's founding documents to be. This is the effect of, and how to respond politically to, rampant industrialization. That it is overlooked is not surprising, given that conventional historical memory regards Management as evolving in partnership with industrialization rather than in response or opposition to it. But looking back into primary sources related to creating and promoting Management before and during 1910, as opposed to after, reveals the role that the problems posed by laissez-faire industrialization in the American political context of the early twentieth century played.

Theodore Roosevelt's record as a critic of industrialization encouraged advocates for big business and their supporters in the Republican Party to lessen Roosevelt's influence by lining him up for the ineffectual position of Vice President. This plan did not, however, account for President McKinley's assassination in 1901. Consequently, Roosevelt became President of the United States at the turn of a new century and at a pivotal moment: a moment in which "the nation suddenly 'woke up' to attend, in its own fashion, to the stress and distress of an industrial civilization" (Fink 2001: 1).

In his first annual message to Congress, on December 3, 1902, Roosevelt subsequently outlined the problem he claimed to be inspiring the work of his Presidency:

> No country has ever occupied a higher plane of material well-being than ours... [While this has] favored the growth of so much that was good, [it has] also favored somewhat the growth of what was evil. [Our] industrial development must not be checked, but side by side with it should go such progressive regulation as will diminish the evils [and] regulat[e] the combinations of capital which are, or may become, injurious to the public.

This agenda put Roosevelt on a collision course with what came to be known as the 'Gilded Age', and its rapid economic development controlled by a small number of commercial 'barons'—men like Andrew Carnegie, J.P. Morgan, John D. Rockefeller and Cornelius Vanderbilt—and what were referred to as their 'special interests'.

As a subset of this agenda, Roosevelt's statements about the need for the conservation of forests have seen him labelled the "earliest environmentalist" (Donald 2007: 164). But the influence of this way of thinking would grow as it came to provide a language that would help counter a growing number of political opponents that began to oppose TR and his allies in what was now being referred to as the 'progressive movement'. Roosevelt's greatest ally in this regard became Gifford Pinchot.

By the end of 1906, influential business interests and political conservatives had organized against Roosevelt's attempts to curb the industrial growth that they regarded as an integral part of the American Dream. Roosevelt had populated his administration with scientists and members of emerging professions like engineering to help make cases for a variety of initiatives towards greater controls and reining in this unchecked expansion. However, these technocrats were more difficult for the public to relate to than the big business rhetoric they opposed (Andrews 2006). Gifford Pinchot was ostensibly only the head of the Forestry Bureau in TR's government, but being a part of Roosevelt's advisory team and realizing that the government's general message had to be sold more effectively, his breakthrough idea, which in his words "put the stone at the end of the club" in 1907, was to formulate and promote a broad "Conservation Movement" (Pinchot 1937: 262ff.):

> The idea was that all these natural resources [under threat from rampant industrialization] which we had been dealing with as if they were in water-tight compartments actually constituted one united problem... We had been dealing with [it] piecemeal, and... not attacking the problem in a united battalion. The idea was so new that it did not even have a name... Finally Overton Price suggested that we should call it 'conservation' and the President said 'O.K.' So we called it the conservation movement.

Pinchot's (1910: 23) definition of the conservation movement's aims resonates with modern definitions of sustainability, sustainable development or Sustainable Management cited as new ways of thinking in management textbooks today. In Pinichot's words it was about:

> making our country a permanent and prosperous home for our children and our children's children... Natural resources must be developed and preserved for the benefit of the many, and not merely the profit of a few.... Conservation means the greatest good for the greatest number for the longest time.

Conservation as an overarching alternative good for America was showcased at a Conference on the Conservation of Natural Resources in May 1908. For the first time ever, all Governors were summoned to the White House to discuss one issue, because, as Roosevelt (in McGee 1909: 3ff.) explained, the question of conservation, "the gravest problem of to-day", had become "so vital". James Hill (in McGee 1909: 64) outlined the stakes in the opening address:

> Of all the sinful wasters of man's inheritance of earth... the very worst are the people of America... [T]he principles of conservation of national resources... must be heartily accepted by all, as the first condition, not only of continued material prosperity, but also of the perpetuation of free institutions and a government by the people... If this patriotic gospel is to make headway, it must be by just such organized missionary work as is to-day begun.

The Conference struck a chord, and Pinchot (1937: 263) was very pleased with its impact: "I know of no similar instance, where a great new idea was introduced to the public in so short a time". Pinchot's pleasure regarding the impact of the event is backed up by the spike in the use of the word 'conservation' in newspaper headlines and headings (see Fig. 3.2).

By 1911, *Moody's* financial magazine could report that: "Conservation, the meaning of which was practically unknown in 1907, has become a household word. [And] the attitude toward conservation of any man in public or private life [now] indicates his stand in the fight for public rights" (1911: 140–141). Roosevelt observed: "The underlying principle of conservation has been described as the application of common sense to common problems for the common good. If the description is correct,

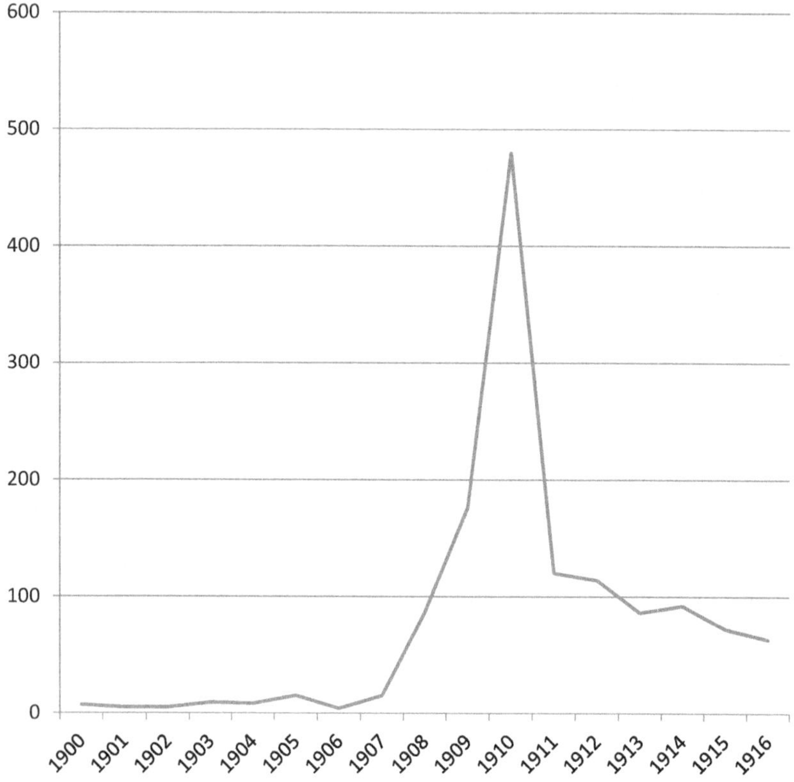

Fig. 3.2 Number of times 'conservation' appears in front-page stories in major US newspapers (Data from the ProQuest Historical Newspapers database)

then conservation is the great fundamental basis for national efficiency" (Presidential 'Special Message' of 22 January 1909).[2]

While conservation had taken shape as a particular project relating primarily to forestlands, the broader movement became Roosevelt and his network of supporters' way to address what they saw as a larger problem. The value of business growth was so intertwined with American patriotism that it "could not with ease be attacked frontally, [it] could [only] be outflanked". And conservation became that flanking manoeuvre (Haber 1964: xii). It provided Roosevelt and his supporters and staff a unified aim that seemed a powerful combination of common sense, science and humanity, one that any householder, farmer or businessperson could relate to.

As Roosevelt would claim (January 22, 1909): "The policy of conservation is perhaps the most typical example of the general policies which this Government has made peculiarly its own during the opening years of the present century". Later social historians would reflect that: "The broader significance of the conservation movement [would stem] from the role it played in the transformation of a decentralized, nontechnical, loosely organized society, where waste and inefficiency ran rampant" (Hays 1959: 2).

Following these initial successes, Pinchot sought to further "unleash… a veritable crusade of enthusiasm for conservation" in order that "a movement peculiar to federal scientists and planners [might become] deeply rooted in the minds of the public at large" (Hays 1959: 122; see also Gerstle 2002). And, for a time, the conservation movement helped turned the tide against Roosevelt's opponents (Harbaugh 1967; Roosevelt 1914: 409ff.).

As Roosevelt left office in 1909, a key strategy employed by Pinchot in keeping conservation in the public eye was to have it feature in the type of prominent legal cases that garnered front-page news coverage at this time in America. And for this purpose, he developed a relationship with a lawyer whose star was on the rise: Louis Brandeis (A.K.A. 'The People's Lawyer').

What would come to be referred to as the Pinchot-Ballinger case of 1910 presented an ideal opportunity to do this. Pinchot-Ballinger was

[2] By efficiency here, Roosevelt in 1909 still means what we would likely call effectiveness. The meaning of the word is still ambiguous at the turn of the second decade of the twentieth century.

not really about Pinchot or Conservation. It was about Louis Glavis, who worked for Roosevelt's successor President Taft's Secretary of the Interior, Richard Ballinger. Glavis informed Taft of what he saw as Ballinger's improprieties in selling public lands to private interests. Taft did not take kindly to Glavis's whistle-blowing and had Glavis fired. Glavis then took this story to *Collier's Magazine* who published it. *Collier's* was then taken to court by Ballinger. Believing that this was an example of Taft and Ballinger soft-peddling on conservation issues, Pinchot leapt into the fight and into *Collier's* and Glavis' corner.

Pinchot recommended that Louis Brandeis be hired to represent Glavis. In consultation with Pinchot, Brandeis set about his work by doing all he could to make the case into a seminar about the virtues of conservation, virtues that Pinchot believed Ballinger and Taft did not share. Brandeis argued that big business interests, in collusion with self-serving government bureaucrats, were seeking to undermine ordinary hard-working young people (like Glavis) who wanted what was best for their future and that of their fellow Americans. Glavis, said Brandeis, wanted to see resources conserved and developed for the benefit of the many not the few.

Brandeis provides an insight into his approach in a letter to his mother (March 2, 1910, Brandeis Papers, University of Louisville Law School Library, NMF 28-3): "The unfitness of Mr Ballinger is being made more and more apparent… Meanwhile the people are led to think about conservation, are learning what it means; and the investigation must prove a very helpful education". Brandeis succeeded in making the case a debate about the goodness of conservation and its connection to a new 'American dream'. His (1914b: xlv) closing argument began: "This investigation has been referred to as a struggle for conservation, a struggle against special interests. It is that: but it is far more. In its essence, it is the struggle for democracy, the struggle of the small man against the overpowering influence of the big".

The case "did indeed result in centring public attention on the vital need for immediate and effective conservation" (Strum 1984: 138; cf. Pollack 1956: 240ff.), leaving Pinchot (1937: 264) extremely pleased with how it "nailed down in the minds of the American people what this conservation business was all about".

3.2.2 *Management for Social Justice*

1910 continued to be a big year for Brandeis's legal and management advisory practice. After the Ballinger-Pinchot case, Brandeis went on to represent the Conservation Association (which had been established by Gifford Pinchot and his brother Amos) in a number of arenas. And, over the summer, he agreed to play a critical role as an advisor in another high-profile dispute: the New York Garment Workers' Strike.

Due to a large number of small establishments, subcontracting, and a largely female workforce that had traditionally not been organized or unionized, the garment manufacturing industry was particularly anarchic and working conditions were poor. But in early July a series of local walkouts had escalated, and this was now hurting retailers. Department store owners the Filene brothers, whose business was affected but held a progressive view of employee rights, began a campaign to get Brandeis involved. "It does not seem to me to make very much difference which side has him so long as one side gets him", wrote one brother to the other (A.L. Filene to E.A. Filene, July 18, 1910).[3]

Brandeis agreed to play a role because his work on other labour disputes had informed him as to the negative social effects of unfair working conditions (he thought these rights and social justice were crucial for conserving human dignity, citizenship and well-being, and what he would call "social efficiency"—Strum 1984: 169).[4] But also because it presented "the opportunity to put into practice some of the ideas he had developed about labor-management relations over the preceding fifteen years" (Urofsky and Levy 1972: 365). Officially he joined to represent the workers' interests, but he acted more as an arbitrator, calling together leaders on both sides for a series of conferences to work out a solution.

There were a number of issues in dispute, but the real stumbling block was the workers' desire for a 'closed shop' (where only union members could be employed) and the employers' insistence on the retention of the

[3] All correspondence from Brandeis is taken from Urofsky and Levy's collections (1971/1972/1973) unless otherwise stated.

[4] As Hapgood noted, Brandeis understood efficiency as a social rather than an economic term. "Considered as part of a social organism," he wrote, introducing Brandeis's ideas, a business "is inefficient if it injures the whole. Even, therefore, if it makes for itself more money than a smaller unit it may be a social liability where the smaller business or institution is a social asset" (Hapgood in Brandeis 1914a: xiv).

current 'open shop' (where they could hire whomever they liked). Brandeis, however, found a middle ground: not a closed or an open shop but what he called a "preferential Union shop"—where employers would have to give preference to union workers if equally skilled union and non-union members applied for the same jobs (Brandeis to L.F. Abbott, Sept. 6, 1910). This solution was a breakthrough, both sides agreed and together with a range of other adjustments (including an independent board to oversee disputes and health and safety conditions), they agreed to a document named "the Protocol of Peace" which was signed on September 2, 1910 (Urofsky and Levy 1972: 372).

The preferential shop was an innovation Brandeis was proud of, and he sought to promote it widely through his media contacts and speaking engagements (Urofsky and Levy 1972: 371ff.). He had developed a significant platform to promote his ideas about business. The publicity created by his work in 1910 had made him "the nation's most famous lawyer" (Strum 1984: 139).

Brandeis then he took on the case for which another innovation—Management as a coherent and generally applicable subject—was formed: the Eastern Rate Case.

3.2.3 *Management for Economic Efficiency*

Within the context of the problematization wrought by a perceived need for conservation and social justice as industrialization advanced unchecked, it was one particular problem, the winning of a specific case in 1910—the Eastern Rate Case—that inspired a particular effort to create Management. Brandeis later claimed he had "no thought of introducing the question of scientific management" as the case began (Brandeis, in Drury 1915: 17). It would be a specific strategic invention developed as the case unfolded.

Just as Roosevelt and Pinchot had used the language of 'conservation' to outline new aims for governing, Brandeis started searching for alternative business-relatable terms to use against the 'special interests' of big business—in this instance, a large railroad company putting up their prices to the detriment of their small customers with no other shipping options. He knew his message would work better if it sounded scientific and appeared to be based on a sound economic logic as well as appealing to greater goods. So his strategy became to show that there was a coherent modern subject that the negligent managers at the Eastern were not utilizing. He subsequently invoked a new argument: reduce waste and conserve resources through applying Scientific Management, the rates can stay as they are and the railroad company's bottom line could grow too. How could any reasonable business person disagree?

This strategy required a solid group of expert witnesses who could present a picture of a robust and coherent new body of knowledge and make the railway executives look outdated for not practicing it. And, knowing the importance of gathering testimony under a memorable banner that named the new subject that could be recalled by the press and the public, Brandeis made this a key consideration at his first gathering of potential witnesses. He remembered having read a book on management by Harrington Emerson which aligned with his own experiences as an advisor to businesses (Lief 1936: 192). He made contact, and through Emerson assembled a group that included Frank Gilbreth, Henry Gantt, Robert Kent and several other engineering and manufacturing consultants.

Everybody in the group knew Taylor's work and suggested their ideas could be related back to his, offering banners for the body of knowledge they were creating such as Functional Management, Shop Management and the Taylor System. Unimpressed, Brandeis intervened: "It seemed to me that the only term that would properly describe the movement and also appeal to the imagination, was 'Scientific Management'" (Brandeis to Drury, January 31, 1914). The others agreed and Scientific Management was born.

The expert witnesses became increasingly important as it became clear that Taylor would not testify. Unusually for Taylor, who had in the past seized opportunities to promote his ideas, he made multiple excuses and claimed to be too busy in a letter responding to Brandeis's requests (November 4, 1910, Stevens Archive, TP58B). However, a note to a friend explains his reluctance in more honest terms. He thought Brandeis's creation "will be so indefinite and vague that it will not be possible to seriously influence [the inquiry]" (Taylor to Dodge, November 8, 1910, Stevens Institute Archive, TP98J). Moreover, Taylor claimed to others that he did not like Brandeis's term, 'Scientific Management' (Copley 1923: 372ff.).

In light of Taylor's refusal to join the proceedings, and to give the subject of Scientific Management (of which Taylor was to be a nominal leader), more weight, Brandeis encouraged his witness team to rapidly create a 'Taylor Society' honouring its figurehead. But when Kent wrote to Taylor to inform him of the idea, Taylor fired back a terse response outlining why he would not endorse it. Gilbreth and Kent then had the delicate task of creating a Society named after a man who did not accept its existence before the expert witnesses took the stand (as a series of letters in the Stevens Institute Archive shows: Box 3).

As the Society was being formed, Brandeis began coaching his witnesses. He trained them well. While the Defence Counsel for the Eastern had Gantt on the back foot at one point, probing as to how Gantt's work could possibly be reconciled with the approaches of the witnesses who had preceded him (Stenographer's Transcript of the Eastern Rate Case: 3477ff. Brandeis University Archive), Brandeis's argument that Scientific Management constituted a unified subject withstood the interrogation.

The next step was for Brandeis to examine the competency (or lack thereof) of the ERRC's executive. Having established that there was a new body of knowledge referred to as Scientific Management, Brandeis then began to reveal a forensic examination he and his legal team had conducted on the ERRC's operations. This was so detailed that it caused well-known railway company President Charles S. Mellen to claim that Brandeis had hired a private detective or engaged some other dubious means to perform such a dissection. Brandeis replied that "Cuvier, the great French naturalist, could take a single bone of a prehistoric animal and construct a complete skeleton. He could do this because of his special knowledge of anatomy. My special field of knowledge is figures. And so I was able to take a few published figures... and working backward, build up their collective system of bookkeeping" (Brandeis, in Lief 1936: 209).

For the purpose of probing executives as he walked them through his analysis of their company, he employed a new term, or at least a new meaning for an existing word. It was not conservation. Rather, it was a word Brandeis likely thought more targeted to expose the executives' lack of business acumen. This was 'efficiency', or doing the same or more with less, as a means of achieving conservation: the sensible conservation of resources, the conservation of effort and the conservation of the small businesses who depended on fair rates to enable them to make a profit.

The novelty of efficiency being used by Brandeis in the hearing is apparent in the stenographer's transcript. One exasperated executive in the dock, confused by Brandeis's use of the term, huffed in response to cross-examination that "you say efficiency I say economy" (Brandeis University Archive, Stenographer's Transcript of the Eastern Rate Case:

2314). As proceedings continued, "Brandeis made it plain that he was taking about a different kind of efficiency" (Mason 1946: 324).

Indeed, a December 4, 1910 *New York Tribune* cover spread about how Brandeis "has set the country about another way of doing things", told its readers that the "bombshell [Brandeis] dropped was labelled 'efficiency'"; putting the word in speech marks and then setting out to explain what it meant. A number of other news outlets did similarly. Even those passing judgement on the case did not seem completely clear about Brandeis's new language. The ICC decision on the case did not even mention the word efficiency, referring only to their opinion that "Something should be expected from [managerial improvements through] the introduction of additional economies" (quoted in Lief 1936: 202).

While Brandeis deployed the terms efficiency and Scientific Management in the Eastern Rate Case, he was quite clear in his thinking that these served the greater good or end of conservation (Dilliard 1941). On November 9, 1910, Brandeis encouraged the editor of the *Indianapolis Sun* to send a reporter to the hearings by explaining: "I feel sure there is no field of conservation which is more important than this" (Brandeis to R.G. Leeds, November 9, 1910). He also kept the Pinchot brothers in the loop, and on November 14, 1910 wrote to Amos: "The time is come when you and Gifford ought to get into the railroad efficiency fight, as the greatest field for immediate conservation" (Brandeis to A. Pinchot, November 14, 1910). On December 17, Gifford sent Brandeis a letter of congratulations about the Eastern Rate Case. Brandeis returned the compliment: "You have so thoroughly trained the American mind to conservation that this new form as presented in railroad efficiency has found a relatively easy path" (Brandeis to G. Pinchot, December 19, 1910).

While a lawyer might not claim that his approach to one case is shaped by others, Brandeis's friend Max Lerner reflected (1939: 80) that his "studies in connection with the Ballinger investigation" influenced his subsequent cases. And according to legal historian Philippa Strum (1984: 168ff.), Brandeis "saw scientific management as a way of achieving conservation" and "his particular approach [in the Eastern Rate Case] appears to have been affected by... the whole question of land conservation". Indeed, conservation as the response to the largest problem of the day and the new good that saw Management studies take form is there to see in the first line of the book that Brandeis (1911: 4) wrote about the case, *Scientific Management and the Railroads*: "The efficiency movement, of which scientific management is an important factor, expresses a new philosophy that conceives of conservation as the central motive in the conduct of industry".

∞

Back in the courtroom, Brandeis struck with the headline making claim that Scientific Management and efficiency 'could save the Railroad $1,000,000 a day' on November 21, 1910. The industry's response was sarcastic. A Railway Age Gazette editorial dismissed Scientific Management as "the merest moonshine" (Mason 1946: 331), and a group of railroad executives sent Brandeis a telegram and gave a copy to the press. "If you can point out a practical way by which a substantial portion of this amount may be saved [we] would be pleased to tender your employment, allowing you to name your own salary. This proposition is made to you in the same spirit of sincerity in which you rendered your statement to the Commission" (November 23, 1910, in Mason 1946: 328).

Brandeis called their bluff. On November 29th in a telegram in response, he wrote:

> I am convinced that such saving is possible through the introduction of scientific management and shall be glad, as a public service, to arrange for conferences... at an early date to point out how scientific management will accomplish these results... I must decline to accept any salary or any other compensation from the railroads for the same reason I have declined compensation from the shipping organizations whom I represent – namely, that the burden of increased rates, while primarily affecting the Eastern manufacturers and merchants [i.e. their customers], will ultimately be born in large part by the consumer through increasing the cost of living... Kindly suggest date and place for conference.

The executives did not reply.

The exchange was reported in the newspapers: "Those somewhat humorous Gentleman will probably regret the levity, not to say the impudence that characterized their communication... Their hilarious incredulity revealed a suppressing ignorance of Mr. Brandeis's record and reputation as a man honestly and disinterestedly devoted to public service" (*New York Times*, November 20, 1910). More tersely, *The Chicago Tribune* recommended that the railwaymen should "drop their tone" (Mason 1946: 330).

The court proceedings followed a similar arc: "The railway cross-examination may be said to have begun in a spirit of flippancy", the *New*

York Evening Post (November 26, 1910) reported, "and ended in a rather awkward silence".

It was clear that Brandeis had won in the court of popular opinion. As the hearing drew to a close in early December, he was heralded in headlines like "Brandeis, Legal Hercules" (*New York World*, December 4, 1910), and "Brandeis, Teacher of Business Economy" (*Philadelphia Public Ledger*, December 4, 1910). By early in the New Year, the ICC had issued their decision. Scientific Management had won in the courts too. In an article in *Moody's Magazine*, Harrington Emerson claimed it a victory for "a new and very simple science" (Moody's 1911: 150ff.). Brandeis's stocks, as a legal counsel and management advisor, soared. As the caption for the cartoon in Fig. 3.3 said, "they all wanted Mr. Brandeis now".

3.2.4 Taylor's Embrace of the Good of Conservation

Meanwhile, what of Frederick Taylor? As described above, Taylor rebuffed Brandeis's approaches to become involved with the trial. While it may seem surprising in hindsight that Taylor chose not to participate, his jaded response is understandable given the state he was in. A little background also helps understand Taylor's willingness to jump on board after reporting on the Eastern Rate Case started to move in Brandeis's favour.

Taylor had retired from his job at the Midvale Steel Factory in 1907 to promote his ideas more widely. He took on teaching assignments and provided talks for anybody who cared to listen. But by 1910 he was frustrated that his system had not become more popular. Even the American Society of Mechanical Engineers, which he had been the President of, was shunning his work. Letters from Taylor to ASME officers pleading with them to publish his submissions become increasingly desperate, until November 1910 when Taylor loses hope (see correspondence in Stevens Institute Archive, Box 60 115B046). In fact, while Taylor's obscurity at this time was forgotten by later interpreters, Kent (1932: 39) reminded people on the 20th anniversary of the Taylor Society, that Taylor's work prior to the Eastern Rate Case "was being ignored". Indeed, referring to Taylor as "an unappreciated genius" in the trial (Gilbreth, in Eastern Rate Case Stenographer's Transcript line 3404, Brandeis University Library Archive) was a necessary device Brandeis employed to explain why this key figure in the new science was so little known.

Fig. 3.3 "They All Want Mr Brandeis Now". Published in the *Boston Post*, February 26, 1911 (*Source* Mason 1946: 328 facing)

Taylor's disposition changed, however, after Brandeis's creation of Scientific Management achieved the desired media reaction. An excited Taylor (in Copley 1923: 369) wrote to a friend travelling abroad to tell him that: "A very extraordinary thing has happened through a Boston lawyer".

Taylor became increasingly enthusiastic about working with Brandeis to promote Scientific Management as a range of publications sought comment from him after the Eastern Rate Case. Brandeis (1914b: xlv) carefully orchestrated the interest and through Brandeis's work, his guidance, contacts and meticulous media management, Taylor was rekindled. Taylor himself openly acknowledged Brandeis's leadership in advancing the subject and his ideas in this regard, noting in a letter to him that he had "w[oken] up the whole country... I have rarely seen a new movement started with such momentum as you have given this one" (Taylor to Brandeis, January 9, 1911, Stevens Institute Archive, TP98J).

As a first step in promoting Taylor, Brandeis encouraged him to talk to as many different magazine writers as possible (Brandeis to Taylor, December 7, 1910), but he also realized the value of granting a longer exclusive to one national forum and steered Taylor towards *American Magazine*. *American* had a wide readership (Taylor initially preferred the high-brow *Atlantic Monthly*), and Brandeis knew that *American* editor Ray Stannard Baker could be trusted to provide a positive spin on Brandeis, Taylor and the new science of Management (Brandeis Papers, University of Louisville Law School Library, NMF 32-1).

Over the next few weeks, Taylor worked closely with Baker on the article draft: a three-part exposition to be published in the March, April and May issues. Taylor's articles would be part of a series that began with a profile on Brandeis's work titled *Brandeis: A Remarkable Record of Unselfish Work Done in the Public Interest*. Here the author would explain (Poole 1911: 490) that "Mr. Brandeis's activity not only had the effect of concentrating public attention upon the [Eastern Rate] case and the real issues involved, but also of creating widespread and unusual interest in the question of scientific management".

Despite initially disliking the term, following Baker and Brandeis's advice Taylor agreed to publish the three *American* articles as a book called *Principles of Scientific Management*. And, like Brandeis, Taylor sought to connect his work to Scientific Management's cause through the greater good of conservation. This helped address what Brandeis had thought to be a lack when he first encountered Taylor's work. While interesting from a technical point of view, Brandeis thought Taylor's writings lacked human interest and any appeal to aims above technical proficiency (Rosen 2016: 48ff.). Subsequently, while many have analysed the content of *The Principles* as Management's founding document, they almost always overlook its initial framing. Taylor (1911: 1) begins the book: "President Roosevelt, in his address to the Governors at the White House, prophetically remarked that 'The conservation of our national resources is only preliminary to the larger question of national efficiency'".

Taylor may have jumbled Roosevelt's actual words (he did not say that conservation was preliminary to national efficiency), but the quotation was broadly correct and its placement in *The Principles* was not so casual.[5] Taylor told a friend that the articles for Baker were "by far the most difficult piece of writing I have ever undertaken. I have had to write and rewrite it eight or ten times to get it into the form which I thought people would be interested in reading" (April 11, Stevens TP185B). And while there is speculation that sections of *The Principles* were actually penned by his assistant Morris Cooke (Wrege and Stotka 1978), a draft of the introduction that draws the connection to Roosevelt and conservation is there in the Stevens Archive (Box 59, file 20b), written in Taylor's hand (Fig. 3.4). It is Taylor that defines conservation as a greater good his work was serving, and Taylor uses this link to provide Baker with a draft that his readers could relate to the concerns of the day. Indeed, while the narrow perspective of pioneering management historians saw the origin of their field in what they term the age of efficiency (as we shall see in more depth in the next section), their hindsight misses that "an age of conservation" preceded this, and that in 1910 and 1911 conservation was "the slogan of the day" (Bodenstar 1918: 12, 337).

Reading the popular business and finance magazine *Moody's* from early 1911 makes this clear. Prominent in the January issue (1911: 70–71) is a review of Van Hise's *Conservation of Natural Resources*: "Magazines and

[5] Roosevelt's actual words in his Presidential 'Special Message' of 22 January 1909 were "The underlying principle of conservation has been described as the application of common sense to common problems for the common good. If the description is correct, then conservation is the great fundamental basis for national efficiency"; later he said: "Finally, let us remember that the conservation of our natural resources… is yet but part of another and greater problem to which this Nation is not yet awake… the problem of National efficiency, the patriotic duty of insuring the safety and continuance of the Nation" (McGee 1909: 12).

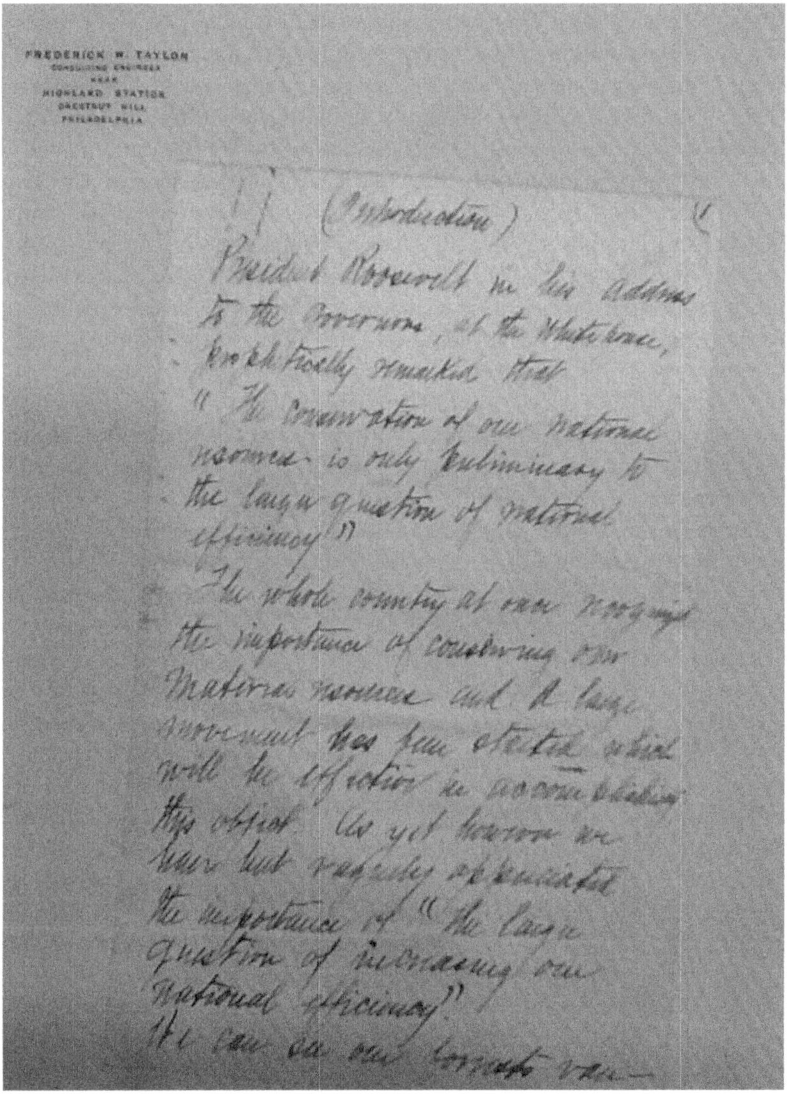

FREDERICK W. TAYLOR
CONSULTING ENGINEER
NEAR
HIGHLAND STATION
CHESTNUT HILL
PHILADELPHIA

(Introduction)

President Roosevelt in his address to the Governors, at the White House, prophetically remarked that "The conservation of our national resources is only preliminary to the larger question of national efficiency."

The whole country at once recognized the importance of conserving our national resources and a large movement has been started which will be effective in accomplishing this object. As yet however we have but vaguely appreciated the importance of "the larger question of increasing our national efficiency."

We can see our forests van-

Fig. 3.4 Frederick Taylor's draft of an introduction to *The Principles of Scientific Management*. Stevens' Institute F.W. Taylor Archive (Box 59, file 20b)

newspapers have been filled with conservation for the past three years", and Van Hise's book is a "practical presentation of the conservation problem... which is at present one of our paramount issues". In February (1911: 140–141), Gifford Pinchot's book *Fight for Conservation* was praised. It was one of a wave of conservation books that entered 'best-sellers' lists at this time, with titles like *Our Wasteful Nation*; *Checking the Waste: A Study in Conservation*; and *Natural Resources and National Wealth*. And Hughes' (2004: 200) sweep of this time in America (much broader than the gaze of management historians) can see that: "Taylor rightly associated his scientific management with the broader conservation movement that had attracted national interest and support during Roosevelt's term as President". Indeed, the archive at the Stevens Institute reveals that Taylor's interest in conservation was not fleeting: he had been a member of the National Conservation Association established by Pinchot in the years prior to the writing of *Principles of Scientific Management*.

Furthermore, despite later writers seeing Taylor as primarily a booster of efficiency as his and Management's greater good or end, he thought the craze of efficiency for efficiency's sake that accelerated after the Eastern Rate Case result misguided. He was adamant his system was "not a device of any kind for securing efficiency"; writing to one enthusiast seeking his endorsement for an efficiency society in 1912: "I hardly know what to say. All the world... wants efficiency now [but] this is not a sufficient basis for a group of men to get together" (Taylor, in Copley 1923: 387).

The focal point of the opening passage of Taylor's *Principles of Scientific Management*, Theodore Roosevelt, was especially pleased with the continued publicity around conservation and the fledgling subject of Management that regarded it as its good. He had redoubled his efforts to conflate conversation and efficiency into key themes in speeches to define a new platform for an attempted political resurrection after he left office. Phrases like: "The supreme political task of our day, the indispensable condition of national efficiency and national welfare, is to drive special interests out of public life"; "Conservation has become a great moral issue in becoming a patriotic duty"; "Conservation is the road to national efficiency"; became motifs in famous speeches at Osawatomie (31 August 1910) and St. Paul (6 September 1910).

TR was also pleased with the Eastern Rate Case result and the rise of Scientific Management (see Donald 2007; Perry 1921). After the case,

Roosevelt further boosted Scientific Management as a means to achieve conservation. He described the new subject as "patriotic", provided an endorsement in Gilbreth's *Primer of Scientific Management* (1912: 2) and wrote an article for *The Magazine of Business* titled 'Scientific Management is the Application of the Conservation Principles to Production'. Endorsements like this from a former (and potentially future) president helped further solidify the new subject as an important concern in the minds of the public.

However, just three years later, in 1915, Taylor was dead. And as the years passed and people referred to his methods without reading his book, it became easier to overlook that conservation was the good that his *Principles of Scientific Management* sought to advance. But seen in the light of how things unfolded at the time, it is less surprising that a review written just after his death (Thompson 1917: 172) places Taylor's work in context in this way:

> The obstacles to the development of scientific management betray their smallness and transitoriness in comparison with the greatness and permanence of the forces with which its progress is allied [in particular i]ts close relationship to the movement for the conservation of all resources.

This context also makes it easier to understand that W.D. Hemmerly, in a letter of commiseration to Taylor's son after his father died, would write (Stevens, 014N001): "it is due to [Taylor's] kind interest in me that I have been as successful... in my attempts to spread his gospel of conservation". It was only later that Taylor's sermon would be defined as "the gospel of efficiency" (Wren 1972: 147ff.).

∞

By the 1920s, as described in Chapter 2, economic efficiency had become an American virtue, both a means and a general end or good in its own right, and a history of management that identified Taylor as its 'Messiah' was emerging (Jordan 2005). Nevertheless, prior to this, people understood Brandeis to be the subject's prime mover. As the Eastern Rate Case was ruled in Brandeis and his clients' favour, and Scientific Management came to be talked about as a new and important subject, it was clear to commentators that it was Brandeis to whom most of the credit should be ascribed.

Tracing reporting in *Moody's* financial magazine in 1911 places the relative merits of Brandeis and Taylor's roles in creating Management in real time perspective. In the March issue (1911: 150ff.), the lead item in *Moody's* is the Eastern Rate Case result. The biggest feature is a collection of opinion pieces on the case, including contributions from Brandeis and expert witness organizer Emerson. April and May's instalments contain articles and letters debating the pros and cons of the Eastern Rate Case and the ICC's findings, and a review of Brandeis's book *Scientific Management and the Railroads*, which is praised for "explain[ing] in the most concise and clearest text we have seen what efficiency engineering, or scientific management, is" (1911: 362–363). The June issue (1911: 440) reviews Taylor's just published *Principles of Scientific Management*: "Of making of books on scientific management there is no end since Mr. Brandeis gave the subject such spectacular advertising in the railroad rate cases, and the general reader may be growing bored by having scientific management stare him in the face so constantly". But it is worth reading, because "[Taylor] is a man who for thirty years has been working out a business system of which few readers... had even heard before the consul for the shippers told the railroads about it publically".

With just distance enough to put some perspective on the matter, but not so far away as to have enabled the repackaging of events in hindsight, a 1913 review, sums up the emergence of Scientific Management in these years as follows (*Railway Age Gazette* 1913, 54[12]: 656):

> the fact [is] that although F.W. Taylor has developed the principles of scientific management for many years, and has presented papers on his work before our great engineering societies, still, until two years ago, he was hardly known, even in his own city. At that time the awakening of the public to the necessity of the conservation of energy and material had made the time ripe for an announcement concerning it. Louis D. Brandeis, in the hearing of the freight rate advance cases, [then] startled the country with it.

Indeed, after losing the Eastern Rate Case, company President Daniel Willard told the *New York Times* (February 24, 1911) that "there is only one thing for us to do—to put into effect the Brandeis greater efficiency system". And, as he continued to represent small-business customers in cases against railroad companies (generally winning by using a similar formula: highlighting how costs would be reduced and benefits to be shared increased through good management) newspapers described decisions in Brandeis's favour as "Brandeised"; and, as his wins mounted, claimed that the ICC had become "practically Brandeised" (Lief 1936: 305). Another journalist reported that "Brandeis created a greater advance in scientific management than would otherwise have come in the next quarter of a century" (Poole 1911: 490). While Brandeis may not have been the first to use the word as a means for managing a business, it was his quest to promote conservation as the central motive for Management and efficiency as a means for achieving conservation that "made efficiency a household word" (Lief 1936: 200).

3.3 The Emergence of Brandeis's View of the Good of Management

> *The efficiency movement, of which scientific management is an important factor, expresses a new philosophy that conceives of conservation as the central motive in the conduct of industry.*
>
> Louis Brandeis, *Scientific Management and the Railroads*. (1911: 4)

If the "counter memories" being promoted in this chapter encourage us to consider that Louis Brandeis could be an important figure in the formation of Management as a subject (Foucault 1977b: 160), we might be prompted to delve deeper and ask how his perspective came to be formed? How did he come to combine his forensic economic analysis of organizations with the conservation movement and ideas about social justice in an increasingly industrial age, to create, promote and popularize Management? The following paragraphs add depth by tracing the development of Brandeis's thinking.

3.3.1 Student, Practitioner, Teacher

Louis Brandeis was born in 1856 in Louisville, Kentucky. His parents were so-called 'Forty-eighters', or 'Pilgrams' of 1848, having fled with many other Jewish families to America from Central Europe during the revolutions and upheavals of this time. His family found it difficult to re-establish themselves in America, but they instilled in their children that higher education and a career in a profession was the way to advance. Louis was bright at school, but deeply disinterested in medicine. An uncle he admired had established a legal practice, and Louis was attracted by the law. This was what he wanted to study, and a determined Brandeis decided that he wanted to study it at Harvard.

There were no formal entry requirements at this time, apart from Harvard's entrance exam—which Brandeis duly passed. But it was expensive. His father was unable to help financially, but Louis' brother Al, several years older but extremely close with his little brother, agreed to loan him $200. Brandeis entered Harvard in 1875 and Al's initial investment, combined with money earned from tutoring work and exam proctoring, sustained him.

At Harvard, Brandeis was one of the first students to encounter Dean Christopher Columbus Langdell's innovative approach of getting students to research and argue particular cases or case studies, including the opinions that Judges wrote in deciding them, rather than just learning laws and precedents. It was a controversial pedagogy that no other University had adopted and many vociferously opposed (Bridgman et al. 2016; Kimball 2009); but it suited Brandeis and has since been adopted by law and business schools around the world.

A need to pay his own way was not the only aspect that marked the young Brandeis out as different. Harvard Law School's other 200-odd students all came from money, but they were also educated at the best New England colleges and preparatory schools, unlike Louis. Brandeis' precocious talent in class also stood out. Then there was the fact that he looked and sounded different. There was a "detectable Southern softness in his voice" and in letters home other students noted rumours that there was "some Jew blood in him" (Lief 1936: 21; Paper 1983: 14).

Another classmate recalled Brandeis in this way: "The pleasant voice of the youthful student, his exact and choice language, his keen intellectual face, his lithe figure, his dark yet handsome aspect, and finally the unaffected suavity of his manner, that had in it something of the Old World Intellect, refinement, and alert and receptive spirit, were written all over his attractive personality" (McClennen 1948: 33).

Brandeis impressed the professoriate at Harvard too, and he was encouraged to continue with graduate studies. He also had the option to settle back in the mid-West and practice law with his uncle. But, after much soul-searching, he went out on his own: staying in Boston and forming a legal practice with his classmate and friend Sam Warren in 1879.

His differences did not hold Brandeis back academically (he finished top of his class), but they were always present socially. When they came to name their practice, it was clear to both partners that despite alphabetical conventions and the fact that the Brandeis's academic achievements were superior, the practice should be 'Warren & Brandeis'. Warren had connections into the upper echelons of society, business and government. And it would be these connections that would build the fledging practice's client base.

Other important connections were also formed at this time. Brandeis married Alice Goldmark in 1891, a partnership that lasted a lifetime. The couple had two daughters to whom Brandeis was deeply devoted. The union also led to another extremely important family collaboration—one that would result in a research partnership with Alice's sister, and the development of Brandeis's signature method of good legal and business practice.

∞

As Warren and Brandeis evolved, it became a hub for some of the most creative legal and business minds in the country: an environment where the "struggles and quarrels incident to corporate organization echoed down the hallways"; where "the relationship of law to commerce" became "a daily fascination"; and where Brandeis became a "student of the strategy of directors" (Lief 1936: 37, 116).

A typical corporate struggle debated in their halls was that of King C. Gillette, founder of the Gillette Safety Razor Company, and inventor of the disposable razor and a business model now widely applied whereby one part of a product is sold cheaply and the 'refills' or 'software' make the profit (Anderson 2010). Brandeis was King Gillette's business and legal advisor, helping him create the Company in 1901 when he had a valuable patent but little money. However, the most significant thing that Brandeis did for Gillette came in the middle years of the twentieth century's first decade. Gillette became concerned that corporate shareholders who were advancing and combining their stakes in the Company were wresting decision-making control from him and curtailing investment in innovation. Brandeis facilitated the development of a holding company, named Inventions Securities Company, in which King Gillette would have the controlling stake. Eventually, the same corporate raiders who saw money to be gleaned from Gillette's inventions, chipped away and increased their stake in the holding company too. But Brandeis had anticipated this. He had set up a holding company for Inventions Securities—the more personal sounding King C. Gillette Company—enabling Gillette to transfer his and his cohort's shares to the holding company's holding company and push ahead with new initiatives without obstruction (Adams 1978).

∞

Given his intellectual abilities, an academic pathway remained open to Brandeis. He was invited back to teach Evidence at Harvard, which he did in 1882 and 1883, but the demands of his growing practice curtailed this. However, his reputation for understanding the workings of commercial enterprise and jurisprudence led Massachusetts Institute of Technology founding President Francis Amasa Walker to coax Brandeis across the Charles River to teach a new course in Business Law at the upstart MIT. Starting in the 1880s, one of Walker's key initiatives as he sought to find a niche in which MIT could compete with the established Ivy League schools, had been to develop a new general and practical course of study (called Course IX) combining economics, English, law, history and modern languages—a curriculum suited to a new breed of professionals and civil servants employed by a growing number of large public and private enterprises (Dunbar 1897; Munroe 1923).

Walker was a kindred spirit, author of an early textbook on political economy and formerly John Hopkins's first professor of economics. He was impressed by Brandeis's holistic perspective of the lawyer's function (which he described as "helping clients not only to understand the law, but also to see their legal problems in the light of their business situation"—in Frey 2014: 117). And Brandeis was attracted by MIT's new, practical orientation. Furthermore, he saw teaching there as a way of providing professional students with a different perspective (he wrote to his father that he "must take up those Institute of Technology lectures to counteract all those monied interests"—Brandeis to Adolph Brandeis, November 30, 1889). So Brandeis took time from his burgeoning case book to prepare a course.

Planning the course coincided with a pivotal moment in the development of Brandeis's philosophy of the purpose of the law and of business. It was the Homestead disaster: an industrial dispute at the Carnegie steel plant in Homestead Pennsylvania, which escalated into a massacre conducted by a security force employed by Carnegie called the Pinkertons. This, he explained in a 1914 interview, "marked an epoch in my own career".

On July 6, 1892, a newspaper Brandeis was reading as he was developing the course carried the story of the pitched battle between the Pinkertons on a river barge and barricaded steel workers on the bank:

> I saw at once that the common law, built up upon simpler conditions of living, gave an inadequate basis for the adjustment of the complex relations of the modern factory system. I threw away my [MIT] notes and approached my theme from new angles... [It was this] affair... which first set me to thinking seriously about the labour problem. It took the shock of that battle where organized capital hired a private army to shoot at organized labour for resisting an arbitrary cut in wages, to turn my mind definitely toward a searching study of the relations of labour to industry. (Brandeis in *The Independent* "Up From Aristocracy", July 27, 1914)

Brandeis steered his course at MIT towards this changed environment.

This moment resonated for Brandeis beyond the classroom too. "Homestead made him a student of economics" and its relationship to the social conditions of workers in industrial workplaces (Paper 1983: 40). The emerging industrial landscape in America enabled men like Carnegie to deploy many new weapons, even a private army. The workers had little means or recourse to respond, and their perilous financial states meant they often faced a choice between accepting an employer's terms or starvation. The scales of liberty had unfairly tipped in the favour of employers against the supposedly free men they employed.

As Brandeis (in Lief 1936: 233) would later reflect, economic servitude was replacing the great sin of slavery, and workers in the new industrial reality were still treated worse than animals or machines. "Every slave was regarded as a piece of valuable property. From a pure self-interest the slave owner would not destroy his property any more that he would destroy his animals". They were cruelly viewed as 'valuable assets' mused Brandeis:

> But... workmen are not [regarded as] valuable assets. They are paid as they go along and when they cease to be valuable... they have been turned off. They went upon the scrapheap, but without that penalty or cost that which comes to an owner in turning a machine upon the scrapheap, because every machine was paid their full value. [Workers in industry] have been paid for the value of their use – and the depreciation charge has not been paid.

Brandeis's professional aims became clearer to him throughout these formative years. He articulated his purpose as being "how to reconcile the industrial system with political democracy" and to determine how the judiciary should help promote a balance "between economic liberty and financial servitude" (Brandeis is Lief 1936: 93, 205).[6]

3.3.2 *Advocate for Better Management*

Sam Warren moved on from Warren and Brandeis in 1897, and Brandeis formed his own firm (Brandeis, Dunbar and Nutter). He continued to develop a reputation as an innovative legal and business mind and an advisor on cases at the intersection of law, business, governance and the civic good. Two public fights helped raise his profile further.

By the end of the nineteenth century, the most hotly contested infrastructure projects that impacted on citizens in the industrializing world were the development of metro railway lines. And, from 1893 Brandeis became an increasingly visible advocate for fairness in the public–private partnerships that built them. When proposals were advanced to place a line through Boston Common, Brandeis opposed it on the grounds that it would denigrate one of the few public parks in the city. In 1897, when the Boston Elevated Railway Company quietly got approval from government for exclusive rights to operate on many of the city's most lucrative routes and keep fares at a set rate for thirty years, Brandeis campaigned against a deal that would "sacrifice the interests of the public to that of a single corporation" (Brandeis, *Boston Evening Transcript*, April 30, 1897—quoted in Mason 1946: 107).

But it was the way in which Brandeis reshaped America's insurance industry that was seen as the first "prototypical Brandeisian reform", utilizing, as it did, his knowledge of law, business, governance and social conditions, and resulting in a solution that others could not see, or derided as "impractical", "wild-eyed", or worse, "socialist" (Urofsky 1981: 33ff.).

The financial well-being of working men and women in Boston and other parts of the US was extremely precarious. Insurance companies backed by venture capitalists looking for high returns, sold income replacement and life insurance door-to-door, safe in the knowledge that very few policies ever paid out. This was because policies would be voided

[6] Brandeis's lectures have recently been published (Cochran 2012); and General Electric President Gerard Swope's student notes from Brandeis's course are in the MIT Archives (Gerard Swope Papers—Box 4).

if just one payment was missed—a regular occurrence when so many families lived hand-to-mouth and there was no welfare system.

Brandeis had to simultaneously work two angles. He had to convince legislators to allow a new type of business to be licenced to enter the personal insurance market. And he had to convince savings banks—the type of business best placed to provide a fair and transparent service to citizens with the financial capital to back it up—to see and take up the opportunity to do so (It turned out to be an extremely complementary opportunity for banks as it introduced them to thousands of new customers). And, much like a tunnel digger, Brandeis had to ensure that both of these angles met at the right place and time. Brandeis pulled it off, much to many commentators surprise, and the kind of income and life insurance that has become commonplace today, which allows some flexibility around grace periods for payments, was born (Urofsky 1981).

∞

Brandeis's private practice continued to gravitate towards business advisory. He was extremely selective in which cases to take on and meetings with prospective clients were famously cursory. The business advisory work he liked presented interesting problems that Brandeis believed he could contribute practical and innovative solutions to. The clients he warmed to were those able to listen and take advice, and flexible enough to change their practices as a result.

Two such clients became firm favourites: shoe manufacturer William H. McElwain and the retail business siblings the Filene brothers, and Brandeis regularly touted their cases as exemplars for the fledgling profession of management. This is how he told their stories to graduating students at Brown University at a Commencement speech in 1912:

> Starting without means, [William H. McElwain] left a fortune... That shows McElwain did not lack the money-making faculty. His company's sales grew from $75,957 in 1895 to $8,691,274 in 1908. He became thus one of the largest shoe manufacturers in the world. That shows he did not lack either ambition or organizing ability. The working capital required for this rapidly growing business was obtained by him without surrendering to outside investors or to bankers any share in the profits of business... That shows he did not lack financial skill.

> But this money-making faculty, organizing ability and financial skill were with him servants, not masters. He worked for nobler ends [and] McElwain made so many advances... that he may be said to have revolutionized shoe manufacturing. He found it a trade; he left it an applied science.
>
> This is the kind of thing he did: In 1902 the irregularity in the employment of the shoe worker was brought to his attention... its economic waste [and] the misery to the workers and the demoralization which attended it. Even in fairly prosperous times the workingmen of America are subjected to enforced idleness and loss of earnings, on the average, probably ten to twenty per cent of their working time...
>
> This irregularity had been accepted by the trade—by manufacturers and workingmen alike—as inevitable... But with McElwain an evil recognized was a condition to be remedied; and he set his great mind to solving the problem... Within a few years irregularity of employment had ceased in the McElwain factories; and before his death every one of his many thousand employees could find work three hundred and five days in the year.
>
> Closely allied with the establishment of regularity of employment was the advance made by McElwain in introducing punctual delivery of goods manufactured by his company.
>
> Dates of delivery are fixed, of course, when orders are taken; but the dates fixed had not been taken very seriously by the manufacturers; and the trade was greatly annoyed by irregularities in delivery. McElwain... insisted that an agreement to deliver on a certain day was as binding as an agreement to pay a note on a certain day.
>
> He knew that to make punctual delivery possible, careful study and changes in the methods of manufacture and of distribution were necessary. He made the study; he introduced the radical changes found necessary; and he so perfected his organization that customers could rely absolutely upon delivery on the day fixed. Scientific management practically eliminated the recurring obstacles of the unexpected.

Brandeis then goes on to relay the case of Filene's Department Stores—an example that might dumbfound the most liberal managers from innovative companies like Google today:

In 1891 the Filenes occupied two tiny retail stores in Boston. The floor space of each was only twenty feet square... Twenty years later their sales were nearly $5,000,000 a year... But the significant thing about their success is not their growth in size or in profits... The pre-eminence of the Filenes lies in the advance which has been made in the nature, the aims and the ideals of retailing.

The Filenes... recognized that to serve their own customers properly, the relations of the retailer to the producer must be fairly and scientifically adjusted; and, among other things, that it was the concern of the retailer to know whether the goods which he sold were manufactured under conditions which were fair to the workers...

But the Filenes recognized... as the common and accepted conditions in large retail stores, that the employees had no voice as to the conditions or rules under which they were to work; that the employees had no appeal from policies prescribed by the management; and that in the main they were paid the lowest rate of wages possible under competitive conditions.

In order to insure a more just arrangement for those working in their establishment, the Filenes provided three devices:

First. A system of self-government for employees, administered by the store co-operative association. Working through this association, the employees have the right to appeal from and to veto policies laid down by the management. They may adjust the conditions under which employees are to work, and, in effect, prescribe conditions for themselves.

Second. A system of arbitration, through the operation of which individual employees can call for an adjustment of differences that may exist between themselves and the management as to the permanence of employment, wages, promotion or conditions of work.

Third. A minimum wage scale, which provides that no woman or girl shall work in their store at a wage less than eight dollars a week, no matter what her age may be or what grade of position she may fill.

The Filenes... have demonstrated that the introduction of industrial democracy and of social justice is at least consistent with marked financial success... The so-called "practical business man," the narrow money-maker without either vision or ideals, who hurled against the Filenes, as against

McElwain, the silly charge of being "theorists," has been answered even on his own low plane of material success.

In examining business cases like these as an advisor, Brandeis favoured an inductive approach developed from researching 'the case' and its context gleaned from his days at Harvard following Langdell's 'case method', rather than deductive reasoning from legal principles as was the norm at the time. Indeed, what Brandeis neglected to tell the students at Brown in this commencement speech, is that it was McElwain's adviser that came up with the notion that the problem to be solved was not hourly wages but regularity of employment. And that McElwain's adviser was Brandeis.

When McElwain approached Brandeis it was to discuss and seek advice about a labour dispute. Unions representing workers demanded a pay rise, but McElwain countered that the wages he paid were above average. Brandeis began where he usually did when advising a client: with a forensic examination of McElwain's books. There he found an anomaly. While McElwain's claim of high hourly wages was correct, the reality was workers only got paid when there was work, and the work was uneven and only undertaken when there were orders to fill—as was the norm. Workers therefore stood idle and unpaid for 10–15 weeks every year. Hence, average yearly wages were low and it was very difficult for workers to plan their finances with any certainty.

Brandeis sought a meeting with McElwain and John Tobin, head of the International Shoe and Boot Workers' Union. Tobin also suggested that irregularity of employment was a problem that McElwain needed to acknowledge, and both McElwain and Tobin were shocked when Brandeis sided with the Union view (Mason 1946; Strum 1984: 97ff.).

Brandeis then urged McElwain to respond by "devising new marketing methods" that would offer benefits to customers if they could spread their ordering, and better organization of production in order to enable a more regular working year for employees (Lief 1936: 88). McElwain agreed. Brandeis saw the resulting organization McElwain achieved through this process as something of an early prototype of Scientific Management (Brandeis University Archive, Box 29, Folder 1: 6–7).

∞

His affection for the case studies of McElwain and the Filenes, brings into focus the perspective of good management that had emerged in Brandeis's mind prior to 1910 and his formation and articulation of Scientific Management.

Brandeis had observed how the rapid industrialization and growth of large conglomerated organizations had created an uneven field upon which the owners of capital and 'the people' now played. "The greatest problem before the American people in this generation", he believed, was "the problem of reconciling our industrial system with the political democracy in which we live" (Mason 1946: 147).

Subsequently, Brandeis was against the 'big businesses' that took unfair advantage of this uneven field: large limited liability companies that squeezed out local providers; irresponsible stockholders and venture capitalists who had no interest other than for an increased dividend or quick pay-out; and against company directors spread across numerous corporations meaning they could only assess decisions in abstract financial terms, rather than in the interests of the particular communities in which those corporations grew. And he was no fan of the special interests of these businesses, stockholders and executives promoted by growing armies of lobbyists. These new industrial conditions were curtailing the freedoms of the working and middle classes: "Is it not irony to speak of the equality of opportunity in a country cursed with [such] bigness?" Brandeis wrote to journalist Paul Kellogg (December 19, 1911). There would "be no deliverance" on America's promise of liberty and social equality, Brandeis said "until the great corporations were curbed" (Lief 1936: 230).

This realization fed Brandeis's interest in labour relations and workers' rights and conditions; his advocacy for workplace democracy and participation in decision-making and cooperative organization; and, in particular, in his seeing the irregularity of work "the most sinful waste of all" (in Lief 1936: 224), whereby workers had little financial security and certainty and no regular leisure time in which to develop themselves and improve their circumstances. But Brandeis was also no supporter of big government intervention, or big conglomerated workers' associations. He was critical of unions governed more by ideology than the realities of their particular members' lives. An orientation that meant, for example, that they were too quick to place all their energies into fighting for higher wages rather than steady work, which would require more local analysis and creative thinking. And it was Brandeis's wariness of big government that would see him back away from Roosevelt and others' approaches to Progressivism after 1911.

By this point in time, Brandeis had developed a position that would confound many observers. In promoting better management for the greater good he would at once be anti-big business, anti-big union and anti-big government. He was against might winning over right in any domain, and wanted to decouple unlimited growth, and a desire for the grand scale, from the American Dream. "There used to be a certain glamour about big things" in this country, he explained, "Anything big, simply because it was big, seemed to be good and great. We are now coming to see that big things may be very bad and mean" (Brandeis, in Lief 1936: 221).

What Brandeis liked was local enterprises, managers who understood that particular business: knowing and caring about the people they worked with, being close to customers and their concerns. He was for what we today would call donut or circular economies, or social procurement, which gave back to communities (Andrews 2015). He was not against businesses making money. He just thought that this money should be distributed more fairly. Hence his opinion that workers should tell manufacturers: "We will join you and make just as much money as possible, but when it is made we are going to have the lion's share of it" while the remainder should go towards capital investment and to the community (Brandeis, in Lief 1936: 224).

Brandeis thought that big, un-empathetic businesses and other power-hungry bodies were also removing a social opportunity that industrialization and technology were enabling: an opportunity for citizens to work less and educate themselves more in an increasing portion of 'spare' time, for the betterment of themselves, their families, their communities, and society as a whole. The regularity of work and conservation of effort that advances in science and technology should afford, would allow people more time to develop themselves into what Brandeis considered 'better citizens'. If he was anti-big business, big government and big unions, he was definitely pro ordinary citizens. It is for these reasons that Brandeis's values were often referred to as 'Jeffersonian'. A Jeffersonian outlook was understood at that time as one that had faith in the masses, and in the idea that, if given the opportunity, most people would seek to improve themselves. In keeping, Brandeis believed in more democracy, greater voice for all, and more authority devolved to smaller local bodies. And it was this cause—better citizenship—that good management and greater efficiency would enable and should ultimately serve (Rosen 2016).

So if it was not big government or big unions that should curb the special interests of big business, what was it? For Brandeis, the best hope for social justice was the skilful development and deployment of the law, in tandem with economics and other new sciences. It was these tools that 'the people's lawyer' would deploy on behalf of the people. But if these were the values and the tools that Brandeis brought with him into his practice of the law, and advocacy for better management on behalf of the clients and causes he sought to defend, what would be the method or process best suited to defend them?

∞

In 1908, Brandeis's previous experiences led him to the approach that would become his signature method—it was an approach that changed judicial practice (and probably management practice too). It was developed to fight Muller v. Oregon in 1908, a case against the exploitation of female workers, and it came to be known as 'The Brandeis Brief'.

Muller's Grand Laundry had brought a case against the State claiming that the Oregon law that forbade him from paying female employees to work more than ten hours a day was an unconstitutional impingement of his liberty. Being knocked back by the Supreme Court of Oregon, Muller went to the Supreme Court.

Brandeis's Muller brief contained 113 pages. But the innovation was that only two pages are devoted to arguments on the law or legal precedent. The rest contain an array of the latest research and statistics pertaining to the physical, psychological, economic and social impacts of women working the kind of hours that Muller was pushing for.

Brandeis had found that similar cases brought to the Supreme Court had been found in favour of employers' claims that laws established to protect workers limited both their and workers' liberty to make their own choices. Through reading their opinions (as Langdell's Harvard case method encouraged), Brandeis (in Mason 1946: 26) could see that Judges ruled this way because legal precedents were shaped by pre-industrial conditions, and because they "came to the bench unequipped with the necessary knowledge of [recent] economic and social science, and... suffered likewise through the lack of equipment in the lawyers who presented the case[s]".

So, if judges lacked the 'equipment' to rule on the actual economic and social conditions of the day, and the impacts that these had on the actual freedom of workers to make choices, Brandeis reasoned that it was the lawyer's job to do the research and present that as equipment that Judges could use.

Having decided upon this strategy, Brandeis called upon his sister-in-law Josephine Goldmark and the support of her boss, Florence Kelley of the National Consumers League (long-time advocates for workers' rights), to help gather the latest research on the effects of long working hours. A team including Kelley, Goldmark and her sister Pauline Goldmark, went to Columbia University and New York Public Libraries to gather up every relevant piece of research they could find. And what they found was organized into the other 111 pages of the 113-page brief Brandeis presented to the Court. Brandeis's brief sought to demonstrate that the Court should accept the research gathered as "facts of common knowledge" and that, therefore, "there is reasonable ground for holding that to permit women in Oregon to work… more than ten hours in one day is dangerous to the public health, safety, morals or welfare" (Brandeis, Muller vs Oregon Brief, 1908, https://casetext.com/case/curt-muller-v-state-of-oregon).

The innovation worked. The state of Oregon and Brandeis won. And, more than this, Justice Brewer, who wrote the majority opinion for the Court, took the unusual approach of naming the advocate in commending "the brief filed by Mr. Louis D. Brandeis". As Oliver W. Holmes (Collected Legal Papers 1920: 180ff., supra note 154, at 187) remarked, the Brandeis Brief replaced the traditional lawyer or justice with "the man of statistics and the master of economics". Brandeis himself summed up the situation with these words: "In the past, the courts have reached their conclusions largely deductively from preconceived notions and precedents. The method I have tried to employ in arguing cases before them has been inductive, reasoning from the facts" (Brandeis, in a 1911 interview, reproduced in Strum 1984: 124–125).

After Muller, Brandeis was involved in a number of other cases and causes relating to workers' rights. He supported calls for better conditions, regularity of employment for workers and minimum wages, and the establishment of a 'Children's Bureau' designed to protect against the maltreatment of young people in the workplace: all against those who claimed that such an approach would be unconstitutional (Lief 1936: 312).[7]

The philosophy behind the Brandies Brief was not especially new—it harked back to Brandeis's Harvard days. But the Muller case brought Brandeis's power for marshalling information and research into a report format to the fore with dramatic effect (Goldmark 1953; Konefsky 1956).

[7] Brandeis continued to work with Josephine Goldmark and researchers associated with the National Consumers League, and through this association became an active supporter of women's suffrage.

Fig. 3.5 "Thus Perish all Patricians". Published in *The Boston American*, May 24, 1908 (*Source* https://brandeiswatch.wordpress.com/2012/05/04/editorial-cartoons-of-louis-d-brandeis/)

Similar cases would never be argued in the old ways again. And while it is well known that the case study method was developed at Harvard Law School, (Bridgman et al. 2016), what is not considered is how the Brandeis Brief became a model for the kind of advisory reports prepared by management consultancy firms that emerged in the twentieth century.

Muller, and the briefs developed by Brandeis in subsequent cases, also harnessed his perspective on the relationship between business and the law that he had developed over the previous three decades. His approach was to persuade jurists that the legal conception of "liberty" should no longer be "synonymous with the laissez faire of Herbert Spencer" (Mason 1946: 581); to help them to see that "[r]egulation … is necessary to the preservation and best development of liberty". This advocacy for mitigating the negative excesses of laissez-faire economics, is an approach that connects Brandeis to the father of economics, Adam Smith, in a surprising way—which we shall explore further in the next chapter.

Between Muller and the Eastern Rate Case, Brandeis was involved in a string of lawsuits against the New Haven Railway Company and other railroads. As these progressed, he tightened the screws against what he and his clients (generally railroad customers) thought were the unfair practices of the large railroad companies and their near monopoly control over local shipping. Brandeis increasingly did so through a combination of forensic accounting and the kind of socio-economic research described above. In so doing, Brandeis became a hate figure for big business executives, and he suffered a number of attacks on his character by executives like Charles Mellen, President of the New Haven Railroad (pictured in the cartoon reproduced in Fig. 3.5 knifing Brandeis in the back).

3.3.3 *Isaiah's Elevation: Management Guru to Political Prophet to the Supreme Court*

During these years Brandeis's celebrity grew. He became a popular after-dinner and conference speaker where he would talk about the law, government and how management and business should develop. After the Eastern Rate Case and Brandeis's introduction of Scientific Management as a new way of thinking about business, the invitations increased.

Brandeis became so popular that he was courted by publishers to produce edited collections of his speeches. This he did in 1914. The book was called *Business—A Profession* (Brandeis 1914b), the same title as the address he delivered at Brown University's Commencement Day in 1912. A transcript of that address was the book's opening chapter, and with the other chapters it formed a kind of 'greatest hits' collection of Brandeis's speeches and essays. In the same year, Brandeis published *Other People's Money* (1914a), a further edition for another publisher on the short-comings of large financial organizations.

Brandeis's books were increasingly in demand because by 1914 Brandeis was recognized as providing economic, business or industry advice to key players in the highest echelons. Having advised Theodore Roosevelt since the fight for fairer life insurance and then the fledgling conservation movement, Brandeis had distanced himself from Roosevelt and his newer political ideas. But he grew closer to Democratic Party candidate Woodrow Wilson (the man who won the Party's presidential nomination ahead of TR). Wilson welcomed Brandeis's council, praising him as "knowing more about both the economics and politics of corporations than anyone else he knew" (in Strum 1984: 197).

Brandeis began discussions with Wilson in August 1912, using his influence to urge Wilson to "make clear to the Country that, in respect to natural resources, as well as human resources, you are quite as determined as the New Party leaders that a broad policy or conservation should prevail" (Brandeis to Wilson, September 30, 1912). During one luncheon and a three-hour conference afterwards, "Brandeis and Woodrow Wilson hammered out the basic tenets of the candidate's business platform, the co-called New Freedom", which became Wilson's manifesto for his presidency (Urofsky and Levy 1972: 661). Strum (1984: 221) goes so far as to say that "without Brandeis, there would have been no New Freedom", and that, as such, Wilson owed a large "part of his place in history to Brandeis".

Brandeis became the "man whose opinion on economic questions [Wilson] respected above all others" (Link 1954: 48), and after Wilson was elected President he came close to naming Brandeis his Attorney General, eventually backing away from such a controversial choice, recognizing "the fact that Brandeis was perhaps the American most hated by big business [and] financial leaders" (Strum 1984: 207; Link 1954).

Brandeis's increasing prominence in Washington's circles of power during the early years of Wilson's administration put him on the radar of those seeking to advance the causes of Judaism and Zionism. Brandeis had not been observant as a younger man, seeing his cultural heritage as more a statement of fact than a state of being. This has led some to puzzle how he could move from this to becoming a leading crusader in the Jewish world. But his biographer Philippa Strum (1984) links the transformation to something that changed in Brandeis in the summer of 1910, directly prior to the Eastern Rate Case, when arbitrating between the largely Jewish workforce and Jewish employers in the Garment workers dispute. Sharing drinks after arbitration meetings, sharing stories about the Ballinger case and less prosaic matters, he felt, for the first time, a bond and an affinity with what it meant to be Jewish and Jewish-American (Rosen 2016). "He discovered during those hot days in August that he was a Jew [and this i]nfluenced his life profoundly" (Lief 1936: 191). It is even mooted that this sudden cultural awakening dovetailed with his thinking about the connection between good management practice and the promotion of social well-being: "From this point on, his ideas on industrial management intertwined with his emotional transformation as a Jew" (Marcus 1985: 202). Subsequently, when he was asked, in 1914, to become the leader of the American Zionist movement he gratefully accepted the offer and served energetically until 1921.

Brandeis was less directly influential in the Harding, Coolidge and Hoover administrations, but through a range of indirect channels provided advice to Franklin Roosevelt and his team on the planning around the New Deal and sought to steer it away from its centralizing tendencies that favoured big business (Schlesinger 1958). FDR regularly but quietly sought Brandeis's council. He came to regard Brandeis as sage, straight-talking and insightful, affectionately giving him the nickname 'Isaiah': the Prophet (Rosen 2016: 1ff.).

∞

These other influential roles notwithstanding, it was as a Supreme Court Justice that Brandeis achieved his greatest honours.

Having baulked at appointing him Attorney General, President Wilson mustered the courage to nominate Brandeis for the Supreme Court on January 28, 1916. But, despite Brandeis's proven legal prowess and his public appeal, the conferral process was fraught and Brandeis still holds the record for the number of days between nomination and being confirmed: 125 (Second and third on this list are Clarence Thomas: 1990, 99 days; and Brett Kavanagh: 2018, 88 days).

What was so scandalous about Brandeis's nomination? Brandeis was the 67th Justice appointed and the first from a religious background other than Christianity, and while this may have played some role in encouraging some in the WASP-ish world of America's ruling elite to organize against his confirmation, it was not the main reason for things being dragged out. The main reason was that Brandeis had developed a reputation for taking the side of consumers, ordinary citizens and little businesses, against big business and big politicians. And those big people had big influence.

Consequently, most critiques levelled at Brandeis were on account of claims he was anti-business and, by seemingly 'taking sides' in this way that he was biased or unconstitutional in his professional practice. Some claimed to the Senate Subcommittee overseeing the appointment that this meant he was "not straightforward" (February 26). Others that he was subsequently not of "judicial temperament" (June 1). The inference was that he was 'dangerous'. But when the Subcommittee asked for examples of these traits levelled against him, opponents struggled to articulate them or backed away when pressed. His fellow justice William O. Douglas later observed that "He was dangerous because he was incorruptible" (see the cartoons in Fig. 3.6).

The protests and cat and mouse games meant that hearings extended across many months. The cartoons in Fig. 3.6 capture the reaction to his nomination: shocked Wall Street plutocrats' faint and others are scandalized as Wilson sheepishly drops the wailing baby Brandeis at their doorstep (Mason 1946: 595). However, 125 days after he was nominated, on June 1, 1916, Brandeis's nomination was approved by the Senate.

Brandeis served on the Court until his retirement, aged 83, in 1939. He died two years later. Despite the fuss surrounding his appointment, Brandeis now appears on almost every list of the greatest ever Supreme Court Justices: an achievement that has now completely overshadowed his work establishing Management.

3.4 Brandeis's Foundations Fade

It is really true what philosophy tells us, that life must be understood backwards. But with this, one forgets the second proposition, that it must be lived forwards.
Often paraphrased to: We live life forwards but understand it backwards.

Søren Kierkegaard, *Journalen* (1843, JJ: 167)

Max Lerner offered this perspective in 1941, just after Brandeis passed away: "When historians can look back and put our time into perspective, they will say that one of its towering figures – more truly great than generals and diplomats, business giants and labor giants, bigger than most of our presidents – was a man called Brandeis" (Lerner in Urofsky and Levy 1971: xxx). In legal circles, this may have come true. More generally,

Fig. 3.6 "The Blow That Almost Killed Father". Published in *New York World*, January 29, 1916 (*Source* https://brandeiswatch.wordpress.com/2016/02/04/editorial-cartoons-about-brandeis-supreme-court-nomination/); "Scandalized". Published in *The Los Angeles Times*, January 30, 1916 (*Source* Mason 1946: 595 facing)

Fig. 3.6 (continued)

not so much—especially in Management. Indeed, as the subject became more established, and then looked backwards to understand where it had come from, Brandeis and the foundations on which he sought to found the subject were not part of the picture.

The paragraphs below explain how Brandeis faded from view as those promoting the subject, object and history of management formed things differently in hindsight. It was partly as a result of Brandeis's own waning interest in Management, and partly because the field sought a hagiographic vision of a founder more in keeping with how the field had developed by the middle of the twentieth century. A founder that could be seen to be both insightful and naïve, and thus built upon as Management 'evolved' in the second half of the twentieth century and beyond.

3.4.1 A Fork in the Road

By the middle of the second decade of the twentieth century, Brandeis's interest in Scientific Management was waning. His legal work was more consuming, but also Management was developing in ways that appealed less to Brandeis's sensibilities. Supporters of Scientific Management had split two ways, and the way least in keeping with what Brandeis thought the profession should be about became ascendant.

The schism had occurred between those who took over the reins of the Taylor Society, promoted by Brandeis in 1910 to support the approach taken in the Eastern Rate Case. On one side, characters like Henry Kendall, Robert G. Valentine and Henry Gantt saw Scientific Management as a technical subject, a tool to be controlled from the top by experts (like themselves and the owners and managers who paid them). It should be the efficiency consultant 'holding the stopwatch', deciding the one-best way (i.e. the most efficient way for the sake of greatest efficiency), and advising managers or business owners accordingly (Wiebe 1967).

But another group, headed by Taylor's assistant Morris Cooke, wanted Scientific Management to be a means to other ends: public interest, social and environmental goods, industrial democracy, conservation, the betterment of society. They believed that choices about the best way forward should come through the involvement of workers. In their view, "Organization from the bottom up not the top down merge[d] efficiency and democracy" (Jordan 2005: 65).

The split coincided with the height of America's enthusiasm for efficiency and America's entry into the Great War, in the last half of the second decade of the twentieth century. As the debate played out in the *Bulletin of the Taylor Society*, Cooke's side complained that Kendall's elevation of the machine and the expert engineer-technician, misunderstood what America stood for: "Germany gives us the example of the mechanistic idea, fully worked out... Is not America's mission to take the measure of that machine and prove its weakness?" (Sheldon and Cooke 1919: 28–29). But it was Kendall's side that gained traction.

Brandeis was disappointed that Scientific Management had evolved in this way. For him, organized labour's dismissal of Scientific Management in the years after the publication of his and Taylor's ideas on Scientific Management was deeply regrettable, but also understandable given that it had become just a tool in the hands of the managers and owners who paid the fees of efficiency consultants who often cared little for social justice and other goods. Brandeis's contention was always that "the purpose [of Scientific Management] was not to speed up the worker but to teach managers to use their brains"; and "that scientific management offered not only social gain – the ultimate solvent – but conservation of human energy and development of the worker's self-respect" (Lief 1936: 222, 341).

It may not be so surprising, therefore, to see Brandeis's interest in the field wane, and his own account of his role in the formation of Scientific Management shift. While they are seldom read today, perhaps the two earliest histories of Management are Horace B. Drury's, published in 1915, and F.B. Copley's, which came out eight years later. Both books acknowledged Brandeis as the key developer and promoter of Scientific Management. And, both Drury and Copley were able to correspond with Brandeis about what inspired this work. But they received quite different answers from Brandeis about his role in affairs.

In the first edition of his history, Drury (1915: 17) reports that Brandeis created Scientific Management in preparation for the Eastern Rate Case after being inspired by a client who owned a shoe factory (i.e., W.H. McElwain). The factory "was operating under the plan to-day known by the name scientific management", and Brandeis was impressed by its operations in contrast to the railroads, Drury reported. Brandeis, in combination with Harrington Emerson, then sought to create a list of and bring together consultants who advised on the kind of principles that McElwain was employing to create a body of knowledge that the railroad executives were negligent for not employing. Brandeis's list of witnesses and how he moulded them into a body of knowledge, in Drury's words (1915: 22), "give us [i.e., students of the history of management] our bearings".

However, Brandeis corresponded with Drury to offer clarification and further explanation as to why the emergence of this thinking was not just based on just his exposure to McElwain—how it was based on his much broader experience as a management advisor. In the second edition of his history, Drury (1918: 17, underlining added) duly inserts the following footnote in relation to the above text:

> Justice Brandeis has advised us that throughout the thirty years of his professional contact with manufacturers and merchants, he had been interested in the questions of improved methods of production... Taylor's paper on Shop Management fell into his hands [after it was published in 1903], and Harrington Emerson had told him of his experiences [applying similar principles] on the Santa Fe [Railroad]. However, [Brandeis made clear that] 'when I entered upon the Advance [Eastern] Rate Case... Emerson's talk and Taylor's paper had wholly dropped from my mind'.

In both of these editions and a third that followed in 1922, Drury (1918: 118) expresses his hope that "Mr. Brandeis's all-important role will not be forgotten". But, just five years later, this was already starting to happen. Even Brandeis' understanding of history was maleable.

By 1923, seven years into Brandeis's term as Justice of the Supreme Court, his recollections had shifted. In a letter to Copley, Brandeis recalled that as he formulated Scientific Management for the case that he "had in mind, among other things, a pamphlet on Shop Management by Mr. Taylor" (1923: Vol. 2: 370–371—underlining added). Indeed, by 1923 with The Taylor Society growing stronger and further away from any interest in conservation, management as a subject becoming more organized, and Brandeis's career having moved into the highest echelons of the judicial world, the title of Copley's book is a clear indication of how history had already morphed in favour of Taylor as the key point of origin, or "the site of truth" to borrow Foucault's (1977a: 144) term. Drury's history was titled *Scientific Management: A History and Criticism*; Copley's, *Frederick W. Taylor: Father of Scientific Management.*

Apart from Brandeis's growing distance from management, perhaps the shift also had something to do with Scientific Management becoming increasingly synonymous with efficiency and Taylor's efficiency 'experiments'. Norman Hapgood, one of Brandeis's most loyal and consistent supporters and friends (Strum 1984), described Taylor not as the father of Scientific Management but as the "father of efficiency study" (Hapgood 1920: 221). But by the middle of that decade, being a pioneer in experiments concerning economic efficiency and being the *Father of Scientific Management* were becoming one and the same.

3.4.2 History Chooses Taylor as 'the Father'

The first, and subsequently most influential, management historian in the middle decades of the twentieth century, was Lyndall Urwick (Urwick earns his place in subsequent lists of the foremost contributors to Management because his histories "integrated" and "synthesized" management thinking—e.g. Wren 1972: 357–358). Urwick was a close associate of Luther Gulick (whose 'basic good is efficiency quotation' began our section on 'The Good of Management' earlier in this book), and together they assembled the *Papers on the Science of Administration*, a "landmark in management literature" (Wren 1972: 355; Gulick and Urwick 1937). Like his co-editor, Urwick was clear that the end that defined management was economic efficiency and that the founder of this approach was Frederick Taylor.

Urwick was first affected by Taylor when reading his work in the trenches while serving in the British Army during World War 1, and he remained a faithful Taylor "disciple" throughout his life (Kelly 1968: 18). Urwick started publishing his historical analyses of management and related subjects in the late 1920s, and his life's work became the twofold process of advocating for management as a modern profession and capturing the history of the field in such a way that it would appear worthy of this status. In this work, Taylor became Urwick's "Galileo": prior to Galileo people thought the world flat; prior to Taylor people thought management to be unscientific and thus not a proper subject (Urwick and Brech 1945: 11). This was Urwick's historical claim. With Taylor in place as the maker and origin point of Management, Urwick embarked on "a lifetime campaign to reconcile scientific management with succeeding schools of thought" (Parker and Ritson 2011: 379).

Creating such an integrated and seemingly evolutionary global history required some bold leaps of imagination. For example, Urwick had to work hard to create a view of Frenchman Henri Fayol (contemporary to Taylor but previously neglected in the United States) as related to and following Taylor's work; and he had to work hard to loop in fellow Englishman Seebohm Rowntree and social education advocate Mary Parker Follett as following on from Taylor, especially seeing as Rowntree and Follett did not concur with this categorization. Moreover, he worked very hard to join Scientific Management and the later Human Relations School, associated with Elton Mayo and the experiments that showed the relationship between being seen to care about worker well-being and productivity, as part of the same tradition (Roper 2001; Parker and Ritson 2011).

Urwick's weaving together of the lives and work of management pioneers such as these into a continuum marked him out as a historian very much of the objective 'great man' variety, and his two best known history books, *The Making of Scientific Management* and *The Golden Book of Management*, were, respectively, collections of 13 and 70 great chronologically arranged influential 'lives' (Urwick and Brech 1945; Urwick 1956). However, none of these lives was Brandeis's. Indeed, Urwick's lack of interest in Brandeis is illustrated by the brief mention in the three-volume *The Making of Scientific Management*. A single sentence on how Brandeis "called popular attention to" Taylor's work (Urwick and Brech 1945: 34).

The one sentence in which Brandeis features contains three errors. The Eastern Rate Case is called "The Eastern Rates Case". The year in which it happened is said to be 1912, not 1910 (an understandable error given that it would be hard to fathom how Brandeis could call attention to Scientific Management before Taylor published his book about it). And Urwick gets Brandeis's name wrong, referring not to Louis but to "Charles D. Brandeis" (p. 34). An error that is repeated in the book's index (p. 180) and not corrected in subsequent editions.

Despite these basic errors, Urwick and his writing were hugely influential, and the effect of his work across the middle decades of the twentieth century was a shared understanding among those who studied Management of a unified and global view of a subject focussed on one universal good. It was just a very different subject and a very different good from that which Brandeis had envisaged.

∞

Buttoning down Urwick's views were three subsequent historians who have the most direct influence on how Management's foundations are portrayed in textbooks and understood more generally: C.S. George,

Alfred Chandler and Daniel Wren. They (especially George who placed an emphasis on a succession of 'great men') furthered Urwick's furrows. Occasionally, Brandeis features in these mid-century management histories, but only in the margins and only as Taylor's water-carrier.

George's (1968/1972) *History of Management Thought* starts with a continuum of 'major contributions to management', with Taylor's contribution significantly larger than any other of the 93 names on the list. Seeking to link Management studies back from Taylor to the most noble of influences prior, leads George to pick out Diocletian, Thomas Jefferson and Jesus as important figures in the management cannon, but not Brandeis or Pinchot or Theodore Roosevelt.

Nor does Chandler see Roosevelt, Pinchot, Brandeis or the conservation movement as important. A summary of his and Wren's viewpoints is well expressed in Chandler's (1973: 393ff.) review of Wren's first (1972) edition of *The Evolution of Management Thought* (currently in its ninth edition). Wren "might have produced a more penetrating analysis if he had focussed on the changing nature of the private business enterprise in the United States ... from a small shop to a giant corporation", as these were "the most critical determinants of the ways in which management thought evolved". In other words, Wren, according to Chandler, would have done better if he had seen history as Chandler saw it (with a focus on the economic context rather than 'great men'). But if one is to focus on individuals, Chandler 1973) agrees with Wren's choice of Taylor as a "central figure".

Wren does not discuss the conservation movement in his history, although he mentions Roosevelt and the Eastern Rate Case briefly as background influences. However, in recent decades, Wren's history has altered its tone further towards a view that sees Taylor as the protagonist in the birth of management as a subject. Until the third edition of *The Evolution of Management Thought*, we are told that:

> Great national concern [that] was voiced by President Theodore Roosevelt and others over the depletion of America's resources ... Taylor who had for three decades fought against the misuse of both physical and human resources, *found himself* as a result of the railroad hearings *the man of the hour*. (1972: 141, emphasis added)

This analysis was backed up with a two-part summary diagram: the first a timeline of the key actors; the second charting the social, economic and political backdrop. The political column lists ‘conservation of natural resources’ between ‘congressional investigations’ and ‘progressivism’ (1972: 271).

However, by the fourth edition of *The Evolution of Management Thought*, history itself had evolved. The second part of the diagram is gone and the quotation reproduced above is changed so as to end:

> Taylor who had for three decades fought against the misuse of both physical and human resources, *gained a wide audience as a result of the railroad hearings*. (Wren 1994, emphasis added)

Written this way, Taylor is no longer just ‘the man of the hour’, fortunate to be in a spotlight created by someone else at that point in time. He has become the protagonist. F.W. Taylor is ‘the father’ of Management.

3.4.3 Brandeis Ebbs Away

The zeroing in on Taylor as ‘the father’ since the 1920s, would have influenced those surveyed in a study investigating the differences between who management historians, business historians and general members of the Academy of Management regarded as their most influential forebears (Wren and Hay 1977). The survey found widespread disparity across the names that populated the top twenty for each of the three groups. But it also found one commonality: Taylor was clearly the number one name in all three sets.

It is this general consensus among scholars of every stripe, and the views of Urwick, George, Chandler and Wren, that come to inform and be cited in the histories represented in the first management textbooks. Under Chandler’s influence, the histories of management that aspiring managers encounter have taken increasing industrialization and efficiency as a key criterion for inclusion; but, perhaps pressed for space and a desire for an easy to follow story, they have been more enamoured by Urwick and George’s approach of stringing together the biographies of great men. Great men and civilizations, the Egyptians, Greeks and Romans, Jesus, Adam Smith and so on, prefiguring Taylor’s discoveries (Charles Babbage, for example, is presented as a “harbinger of the new scientific management”—George 1972: 76–77; Urwick and Brech 1945: 24ff.). Then, later Management thinkers and schools, following Urwick’s analysis, build upon Taylor as the hinge joining past and future.

Economic efficiency, as the good of Management, is thus understood as a natural, pre-existing object, which some earlier civilizations may have partially understood, but it is Taylor who is the keystone because he recognized the universal importance of efficiency and explicitly promoted it above anything else. Because these histories provided the foundational perspective for so many of those management textbooks that emerged in the late twentieth century, (textbooks that still dominate the market forty years later, in their umpteenth editions), and because popular management authors and critical management scholars alike have stopped questioning the strawman version of Taylor's primary status in creating Management studies, this consensus has become increasingly 'baked into' to minds of recent generations of management scholars, practitioners and protagonists.

At the same time, any recognition given to Brandeis has dwindled. While Wren's earlier editions of *The Evolution* describe him as a minor contributor (1972: 182–183), by the fourth edition, this and references to books by and about Brandeis have disappeared. Brandeis fades, and Taylor becomes—unequivocally—the man who made Management.

As a consequence, in 1976, Peter Drucker (1981: 96), with a little research, could still make the following claims challenging Management's newly formed historical assumptions:

> Everybody "knows" the following "facts" about Frederick Winslow Taylor: His "aim" was "efficiency", which meant reducing costs and increasing profits. He believed that workers responded primarily to economic incentives... He considered workers to be "machines" and to be used as machines. He wanted to put all power and control into the hands of management... But even the most cursory reading of Taylor immediately shows that everyone on these "well-known facts" is pure myth.

But just a few decades later, this generation's equivalents to Drucker find it harder to see beyond Management's conventional historical bounds: "as managers we are captives of a paradigm that places the pursuit of efficiency ahead of every other goal. This is hardly surprising, since modern management was invented to solve the problem of inefficiency" (Hamel 2007: 12ff.).

Indeed, it is now, in the twenty-first century, very hard to think past efficiency as Management's fundamental good and Taylor as its founder. As more and more of the historical record from the time when Scientific Management was created lies buried in archives or is lost, and new generations of researchers look at secondary sources and digitized content, seeing all the way back to what happened at the beginning of the twentieth century rather than what management historians in the middle of the twenty-first century wanted to see is a difficult task.

Making it harder still to see back to Brandeis's work on Management and how thinking about social and environmental well-being played a foundational role in his thinking, is the fact that those who are critical of accepted management conventions at the same time uncritically adhere to the 'Taylor was the man who made Management' narrative. Braverman (1974), for example, follows Chandler's marks, while more recent texts like Fulop and Linstead's (1999: 210ff.) describe Taylor as having "coined the term" Scientific Management. Morgan's unconventional textbook *Images of Organization* (2006) uniquely provides a historical perspective as a general backbone, but the narrative is the same: Management begins with Taylor employing the mechanistic gaze of economic efficiency.

Monin's (2012: 92ff.) critique, unaware of the network of relations between Taylor and the conservation movement, takes Taylor to task for his insincerity, audacity and opportunism in seeking to link his work to the noble cause of conservation at the beginning of *Principles of Scientific Management*. Indeed, by the second decade of the twentieth century, having been taught for so long that Taylor was solely focussed on economic efficiency at the expense of the well-being of employees and the environment, it's hard to get one's head around the fact that what we think is a modern concern: conservation or sustainability, was a real and genuine concern in his mind and in the minds of the founders of Management.

∞

As decades pass, it is harder to get behind what Foucault (1977a: 144) called the "long baking process" of history and see the influence of Louis Brandeis on an earlier incarnation of Management than what we consider the original. As Max Lerner's prophesy about our memory of Brandeis (described earlier) has only come true in legal circles, remembrances of and the records we keep about him are increasingly skewed to seeing Brandeis's legacy as limited to that realm. The University of Louisville Brandeis Archive does not list his *Scientific Management and the Railroads* (1911) among his published books. A recent one-hour documentary about Brandeis's life is well made, but says nothing about the Eastern Rate Case and Brandeis's role as a management advisory and creator of Scientific Management.[8] And it is not easy to find records of Brandeis's management advisory work or copies of his Management books like *Business—A Profession*. Unless we make a concerted effort now, Brandeis's foundations of good Management: conservation, social goods like citizenship and community engagement, and economic efficiency advanced collectively, will be lost: more and more difficult to see behind the mountain of 'evolving' Management approaches piling up in the annals and promoted by the textbooks.

References

Adams, R. 1978. *King C. Gillette: The man and his wonderful shaving device*. Boston, MA: Little, Brown.

Anderson, C. 2010. *Free: The future of a radical price*. New York: Cornerstone.

Andrews, D. 2015. The circular economy, design thinking and education for sustainability. *Local Economy* 30 (3): 305–315.

Andrews, R.N. 2006. *Managing the environment, managing ourselves: A history of American environmental policy*. New Haven, CT: Yale University Press.

Bodenstar, W.H. 1918. *The Journal of the American Medical Association*, 12.

Brandeis, L.D. 1911. *Scientific management and the railroads*. New York: Engineering.

Brandeis, L.D. 1914a. *Other people's money and how the bankers use it*. Harper's.

Brandeis, L.D. 1914b. *Business: A profession*. New York: Small, Maynard & Co.

Braverman, H. 1974. *Labor and monopoly capital: The degradation of work in the twentieth century*. New York: NYU Press.

Bridgman, T., S. Cummings, and C. McLaughlin. 2016. Re-stating the case: How revisiting the development of the case method can help us think differently about the future of the business school. *Academy of Management Learning and Education* 15 (4): 724–741.

Callender, G. 2008. *Efficiency and management*. London: Routledge.

Chandler, A.D. 1973. Review of the evolution of management thought by Daniel A. Wren. *Business History Review* 47 (3): 393–395.

Clark, C.M.A. 1992. *Economic theory and natural philosophy: The search for the natural laws of the economy*. Aldershot: Edward Elgar.

Cochran, R.F. 2012. *Louis D. Brandeis's MIT lectures on law (1892–1894)*. Durham, NC: Carolina Academic Press.

Copley, F.B. 1923. *Frederick W. Taylor: Father of scientific management*, vol. 2. New York: NY: Harper.

Cummings, S. 2002. *Recreating strategy*. London: Sage.

Dilliard, I. 1941. *Mr. Justice Brandeis*. St. Louis: Modern View.

[8] https://www.brandeis.edu/ldb-100/multimedia.html.

Donald, A.D. 2007. *Lion in the White House: A life of Theodore Roosevelt*. New York: Basic Books.
Drucker, P.F. 1981. The coming rediscovery of scientific management. Reproduced in *Toward the next economics, and other essays* (pp. 96-105) New York: Harper Collins.
Drury, H.B. 1915/1918. *Scientific management: A history and criticism*. New York, NY: Columbia.
Dunbar, W.H. 1897. Government by injunction. *LQ Rev.* 13: 347.
Fink, L. 2001. *Major problems in the gilded age and progressive era*. Boston: Houghton-Mifflin.
Foucault, M. 1970. *The order of things: An archaeology of the human sciences*. London: Tavistock.
Foucault, M. 1977a. *Discipline and punish: The birth of the prison*. London: Allen Lane.
Foucault, M. 1977b. *Language, counter-memory, practice*. Ithaca, NY: Cornell University.
Foucault, M. 1985. *The history of sexuality: Volume two—The use of pleasure*. New York: Pantheon.
Frey, R.M. 2014. Review of Cochran, R.F. 2012. *Louis D. Brandeis's MIT lectures on law. The Federal Lawyer*, May/June, pp. 117–118.
Fulop, L., and S. Linstead. 1999. *Management: A critical text*. London, UK: Macmillan Education.
George, C.S. 1968/1972. *The history of management thought*, 1st/2nd ed. Englewood Cliffs, NJ: Prentice Hall.
Gerstle, G. 2002. *American crucible: Race and nation in the twentieth century*. Princeton: Princeton University Press.
Gilbreth, F.B. 1912. *Primer of scientific management*. New York: Van Nostrand.
Goldmark, J. 1953. *Impatient crusader*. Urbana: University of Illinois Press.
Gordon, R.J. 2017. *The rise and fall of American growth: The US standard of living since the civil war*. Princeton: Princeton University Press.
Gray, H., and S. Turner. 1916. *Eclipse or empire?*. London: Nisbet & Co.
Gulick, L.H., and L.F. Urwick (Eds.). 1937. *Papers in the science of administration*. New York: Columbia University Press.
Haber, S. 1964. *Efficiency and uplift: Scientific management in the progressive era 1890–1920*. Chicago: University of Chicago Press.
Hamel, G. 2007. *The future of management*. Brighton: Harvard Business Press.
Hapgood, N. 1920. *The advancing hour*. New York: Boni & Liveright.
Harbaugh, W.H. 1967. *The life and times of Theodore Roosevelt*. New York: Collier.
Hays, S.P. 1959. *Conservation and the gospel of efficiency: The progressive conservation movement, 1890–1920*. Cambridge: Harvard University Press.

Holmes, O.W. 1920. *Collected legal papers*. New York: Harcourt, Brace and Howe.
Hughes, T.P. 2004. *American genesis: A century of invention and technological enthusiasm, 1870–1970*. Chicago: University of Chicago Press.
Jordan, J.M. 2005. *Machine-age ideology: Social engineering and American liberalism, 1911–1939*. Chapel Hill, NC: University of North Carolina Press.
Kelly, J. 1968. *Is scientific management possible?*. London: Faber & Faber.
Kent, R.T. 1932. The Taylor Society twenty years ago. *Bulletin of the Taylor Society* 17: 39–41.
Kierkegaard, S. 1843. *Søren Kierkegaard's Skrifter*. Copenhagen: Copenhagen University.
Kimball, B.A. 2009. *The inception of modern professional education: C. C. Langdell, 1826–1906*. Chapel Hill: University of North Carolina Press.
Konefsky, S.J. 1956. *The legacy of Holmes and Brandeis: A study on the influence of the ideas*. New York: Collier.
Koontz, H. 1980. The management theory jungle revisited. *Academy of Management Review* 5: 175–188.
Lerner, M. 1939. *Ideas are weapons: The history and uses of ideas*. New York: Transaction.
Lief, A. 1936. *Brandeis: The personal history of an American ideal*. Telegraph: Pittsburg, PA.
Link, A.S. 1954. *Woodrow Wilson and the progressive era*. New York: Harper and Brothers.
Marcus, M. 1985. Falling under the Brandeis Spell. *The Yale Law Journal* 95 (1): 195–206.
Mason, A.T. 1946. *Brandeis: A free man's life*. New York: Viking.
McClennen, E.F. 1948. Louis D. Brandeis as a lawyer. *Massachusetts Law Quarterly* 33 (1): 22–23.
McGee, W.J. 1909. *Proceedings of a conference with Governors*. Washington, DC: Government Printing Office.
Monin, N. 2012. *Management theory: A critical and reflexive reading*. London and New York: Routledge.
Moody's Magazine. 1911. *The international investors' monthly*, vol. XI. New York: Ferrin.
Morgan, G. 2006. *Images of organization*. Thousand Oaks, CA: Sage.
Munroe, J.P. 1923. *A life of Francis Amasa Walker*. New York: H. Holt.
Oxford English Dictionary. 1989. *Greater Oxford English Dictionary*. Oxford: Oxford University Press.
Paper, L.J. 1983. *Brandeis: An intimate biography of one of America's truly great Supreme Court justices*. Englewood Cliffs, NJ: Prentice Hall.

Parker, L.D., and P. Ritson. 2011. Rage, rage against the dying of the light: Lyndall Urwick's scientific management. *Journal of Management History* 17 (4): 379–398.

Perry, B. 1921. *Life and letters of Henry Lee Higginson*. Boston: Atlantic.

Pinchot, G. 1910. *The fight for conservation*. New York: Doubleday.

Pinchot, G. 1937. How conservation began in the United States. *Agricultural History* 11: 255–265.

Pollack, E.H. 1956. *The Brandeis reader*. New York: Oceana.

Poole, E. 1911. Brandeis: A remarkable record of unselfish work done in the public interest. *American Magazine*, February, pp. 481–493.

Roosevelt, T.D. 1914. *Theodore Roosevelt—An autobiography*. New York: Macmillan.

Roper, M. 2001. Masculinity and the biographical meanings of management theory: Lyndall Urwick and the making of scientific management in inter-war Britain. *Gender, Work and Organization* 8 (2): 182–204.

Rosen, J. 2016. *Louis D. Brandeis: American prophet*. New Haven: Yale University Press.

Schlesinger, A.M. 1958. *The coming of the new deal: 1933–1935*. The age of Roosevelt. Boston: Houghton Mifflin Harcourt.

Seldes, J. 1917. American efficiency in England. *Bellman* 22: 122–123.

Sheldon, O., and M. Cooke. 1919. Discussion. *Bulletin of the Taylor Society* 4: 28–29.

Strum, P. 1984. *Louis D. Brandeis: A Justice for the people*. New York: Schocken Books.

Taylor, F.W. 1911. *The principles of scientific management*. New York: Harper & Row.

Thompson, C.B. 1917. *The theory and practice of scientific management*. Boston: Houghton Mifflin.

Urofsky, M.I. 1981. *Louis D. Brandeis and the progressive tradition*. Boston, MA: Little, Brown.

Urofsky, M.I., and D.W. Levy. 1971/1972/1973. *Letters of Louis D. Brandeis*, vols. I, II, III. Albany, NY: State University of New York Press.

Urwick, L.F. 1956. *The golden book of management: A historical record of the life and work of seventy pioneers*. London: N. Neame.

Urwick, L.F., and E.F.L. Brech. 1945. *The making of scientific management—Volume 1: Thirteen pioneers*. London: Pitman.

Veblen, T. 1904. *The theory of business enterprise*. New York: Scribner's Sons.

Wiebe, R.H. 1967. *The search for order, 1877–1920*. London: Macmillan.

Wrege, C.D., and A.M. Stotka. 1978. Cooke creates a classic: The story behind F. W. Taylor's principles of scientific management. *Academy of Management Review*, 3 (4): 736–49.

Wren, D.A. 1972/1994. *The evolution of management thought*, 1st/4th ed. New York: Ronald Press.

Wren, D.A., and R.D. Hay. 1977. Management historians and business historians: Differing perceptions of pioneer contributors. *Academy of Management Journal* 20 (3): 470–476.

CHAPTER 4

A New History of (Sustainable) Management

Abstract Our counter-history has questioned assumed continuities and discontinuities that inform our historical understanding of Management and Sustainable Management: Taylor was not a miraculous break from the past, the adoption of his ideas was part of a broader age of conservation; Management did not evolve to support an industrial world view, but in opposition to it; Sustainable Management is not a new breakthrough, but a continuous concern since pre-modern times. Thinking differently in this way enables us to propose a new history: one where Sustainable Management is not an add-on to Management, but where they are one and the same. It is a new history linking indigenous approaches: Smith's *Theory of Moral Sentiments*, Brandeis, Mary Parker Follett and a diverse range of Management founders. In this way, sustainability can be seen at the core of Management: a key point of origin defining a different fundamental good for Management in the present and for the future.

Keywords Indigenous Peoples · Adam Smith · Theory of Moral Sentiments · Mary Parker Follett · Sustainable Development Goals

S. Cummings and T. Bridgman, *The Past, Present and Future of Sustainable Management*,
https://doi.org/10.1007/978-3-030-71076-7_4

In an interview published under the title *History of the Present*, Michel Foucault (1988: 13) argued that "What is good is something that comes through innovation". Elaborating, he explained that contrary to what we might be led to believe, "The good does not exist... in an atemporal sky, with people who would be like the Astrologers of the Good, whose job is to determine what is the favorable nature of the stars".

"The good", Foucault concluded hopefully, "is defined by us, it is practiced, it is invented. And this is a collective work."

The history of Management (and by association the good of management) could have been invented in different ways. If it had seen Brandeis as a founder, then the good of management could have been conservation, or the kind of things that Brandeis and his network linked the achievement of conservation too. Efficiency, as an economic ratio, would have been a useful component, but as a means to reduce waste and the impact on the natural environment and enabling greater social, environmental, cultural and civic well-being. Instead, by the middle decades of the twentieth century, a history had emerged that defined the good and the end of management as increasing economic efficiency.

For Brandeis, efficiency was about doing the same, or a little more, with less, so as to enable more time, resources and consideration for improving well-being. It was a means to other ends: individual well-being through education and a more balanced existence through improved leisure, greater social connections and time spent in nature; but also collective well-being, stronger communities and better civic engagement. For Brandeis, efficiency was "subsidiary to the broader goal [, the] ultimate goal was to promote not efficiency but democracy" (Rosen 2016: 51, 76).

As Henry Gantt and those who led Management down a different path saw things: "The increase of this efficiency is essentially the problem of the manager, and the amount to which it can be increased... is... so great as to be almost incredible" (Gantt 1911: 14). And for Gantt, "The aim of our efficiency has not been to produce goods, but to harvest dollars... The production of goods was always secondary to the securing of dollars" (Gantt, in Polakov 1922: 152, by goods he means products here, but we can see how financial measures of efficiency are taking hold).

For those who took Scientific Management this way, it came to be about doing a lot more with less, or with more (and more), so long as the margins between costs and outputs grew wider, and profits, surpluses, and financial dividends grew greater and greater. And this led to a treadmill, a hamster wheel with no end, which rather than enhancing social and environmental well-being ate away at it.

Philosopher Alasdair MacIntyre (1984) developed a conception that expresses the rationality associated with this view of the good of management: a circular 'bureaucratic rationality', where economic efficiency is both the end aimed for *and* the means to achieve this end. And because this worldview lacks any greater good, and is instead subservient to efficiency—a means posing as an end—MacIntyre and other scholars claimed that Management could never really become a 'true' profession like medicine or architecture (Kavanagh 2013).

Furthermore, we would argue, this pathway for Management cannot have sustainability at its heart. It can only be an add-on in this scenario. To help Management to be more, to see Management and Sustainable Management as part of the same enterprise, it would be useful to turn back, to understand and retrace our steps back to the fork in the road.

The fork we need to look back to occurred in the second decade of the twentieth century. Prior to this, conservation was probematized in America; after this, greater economic efficiency became both a means for improvement in almost every pursuit and a general good in its own right. Prior to this, Brandeis devoted a great deal of his energy to founding management as a profession; after this his energies were directed elsewhere. Prior to this, Taylor was alive to promote his own legacy. And, prior to this, efficiency had different meanings.

A decade earlier, efficiency was a pseudonym for effectiveness. Theodore Roosevelt in 1900 could equate it to the general act of achieving success or practical results, whatever one wished the goods that denoted success to be.[1] In the years around 1910, conservation and efficiency (the way that Brandeis and others conceived it) were compatible: allied rather than opposed. They both came from similar etymological roots, adapted from natural philosophy where they had been used as measures of effective energy and force by the likes of Colding, Joule and Faraday. Both words focused attention on reducing waste for the purposes of advancing other goods. Efficiency led to conservation and conservation

[1] "These two attitudes, the attitude of deifying mere efficiency, mere success, without regard to the moral qualities lying behind it, and the attitude of disregarding efficiency, disregarding practical results, are the Scylla and Charybdis between which every[one] must steer" Roosevelt, in Latitude and Longitude among Reformers, *The Strenuous Life: Essays and Addresses* (1900).

led to more to enjoy for more people: more time, more nature, more community, more education. But, by the middle of the decade, efficiency was increasingly seen as a ratio and understood as a good in its own right, with monetary units rather than energy becoming the proxy for cost and product. Looking back later in the twentieth century, management historians defined this as both a universal and timeless object of concern and the good that defined their subject.

If we were to pin a year to the crux, it might be 1916: one year after Taylor died, the year Brandeis became a member of the Supreme Court, and the year before the recorded spike in the use of the word efficiency as it developed its new meaning. A spike described as a flash flood, one that contributed to washing the good of conservation to the margins (Haber 1964).

Like Brandeis, philosopher John Dewey saw goods other than economic efficiency as what we should be working towards. For example, he named increasing 'social efficiency' as a key aim of education. It is a term odd to our eyes, one that Dewey (1911, in Knoll 2009: 377) had taken from an earlier time and which he defined as the "increasing of ability to share in the appreciation and enjoyment of all values of social inter-course". And in 1916, conscious of the way in which discussion about the practice of Scientific Management was developing, Dewey observed in his influential book *Democracy and Education* that:

> Much is said about scientific management of work. It is a narrow view which restricts the science which secures efficiency of operation to movements of the muscles. The chief opportunity for science is the discovery of the relations of a man to his work — including his relations to others who take part — which will enlist his intelligent interest in what he is doing. Efficiency in production often demands division of labor. But it is reduced to mechanical routine unless workers see the technical, intellectual, and social relationships involved in what they do, and engage in their work because of the motivation furnished by such perceptions. The tendency to reduce such things as efficiency of activity and scientific management to purely technical externals is evidence of the one-sided stimulation of thought given to those in control of industry — those who supply its aims. Because of their lack of all-round and well-balanced social interest, there is not sufficient stimulus for attention to the human factors and relationships in industry. Intelligence is narrowed to the factors concerned with technical production and marketing of goods. No doubt, a very acute and intense intelligence in these narrow lines can be developed, but the failure

> to take into account the significant social factors means none the less an absence of mind, and a corresponding distortion of emotional life. (Dewey 1916: 98–99)

The history of Management, the subsequent layering up of new schools of thought and the way Management's invented origins came to be uncritically repeated, have covered the tracks back to and around this branching off point. The counter-history in the previous chapter was a kind of archaeological survey to resurface them, and by so doing to help begin "free our thought from what it silently thinks"—to paraphrase Michel Foucault—about the good of management, to provide some space for us to reinvent the subject's good and, subsequently, to encourage practicing management differently.

The rest of this chapter seeks to develop a new history to inspire future development. A history in which Sustainable Management and Management in general, have common goods at their roots. It is for this reason that the title of the chapter has Sustainable in brackets. For in this new history Management and Sustainable Management are no longer distinct: the latter no longer an appendage to the former. They are one.

It begins by summarizing the case for Louis Brandeis to be considered a founder of the field, a new link or hinge between our past and future, a case for his work not Taylor's to be Management's origin. And then it traces a lineage before this point and from this point to the present.

4.1 The Case for Another Origin

> *As the profession of business develops, the great industrial and social problems expressed in the present social unrest will one by one find solution.*
>
> Louis Brandeis, *Business—A Profession.* (1914b)

Positioning Louis Brandeis as a founder of Management seems far-fetched, particularly for those inculcated with Management's conventional history. But, if you look closely at Brandeis against Taylor, Brandeis appears a better option on many measures (see Fig. 4.1).

Both developed principles of good management and business that would be organized under the banner of 'Scientific Management', Management's first school of thought. But it was Brandeis, not Taylor,

	Taylor	*Brandeis*
Developed principles grouped under Scientific Management banner:	Yes	Yes
Developed the term Scientific Management:	No	Yes
First to popularise Management:	No	Yes
First to publish book titled Scientific Management:	No (April, 1911)	Yes (1911, February)
First taught business at a University:	1907, Harvard	1892, MIT
Innovative method:	Shop management principles	'Brandeis Brief'
Number of clients:	Dozens	Hundreds
No. of US Presidents advised:	0	3
Advocate for management as a profession	Not particularly	Yes

Fig. 4.1 Founder of management: Frederick Taylor vs Louis Brandeis

who sought to develop Management as a subject made up of many different leading thinkers and practitioners. It was Brandeis who developed the term Scientific Management. It was Brandeis who was first to promote the idea of Management as a subject to be taken seriously in the last months of 1910. And Brandeis was the first to publish a book with Scientific Management in the title (*Scientific Management and the Railroads*, in February of 1911).

Taylor appears to have thought what he had to offer more appropriate for engineering schools rather than schools of business, but he did teach a course at Harvard from 1909. The title of Taylor's course is recorded in histories now as 'Scientific Management' (Kakar 1970: 174), but, the actual title of Taylor's course was Workmen and Their Management (remember 1909 is a year prior to Brandeis inventing the term Scientific Management). Brandeis taught his paper, Business Law—what we might call a 'management in the business environment' course, at MIT 15 years earlier. Both ran business advisory practices, but whereas Taylor's clients numbered dozens, Brandeis advised hundreds from small-business owners to three presidents of the United States. Both Taylor and Brandeis developed case studies. Taylor's famous (although now regarded as fictional—Wrege and Peroni 1974), story of a workman called Schmidt shovelling under instruction from Taylor, is taught to students to this day: despite seeming far more innovative and relevant Brandeis's cases about the Filene brothers and William McElwain never are.

Both Brandeis and Taylor developed what we might today call a 'signature approach'. Taylor his 'Principles'; Brandeis 'The Brief'. The Brandeis Brief advocated seeking to understand particular cases by placing them in sociological and economic context, and its focus on researched facts and figures became a template for professional jurisprudence and business advisory in the twentieth century. Indeed, in the case of Liggett vs. Lee Brandeis's Brief offered an entire history of the corporation in the course of America's development, which is interesting to read alongside Chandler's more well-known histories. In utilizing his craft and tools like the Brief, Brandeis was not so much an attorney as a "counsel to the situation"; or "a kind of Jeffersonian McKinsey Consultant representing the interests of both labor and management… [I]mmersing himself in the facts… attempt[ing] to identify what both sides wanted and propose creative solutions that balanced all of the interests concerned" (Urofsky 1981: 146; Rosen 2016: 44, 111).

Finally, Brandeis spent many years actively promoting Management and how the profession should be seen. Taylor promoted his own techniques and principles, but by contrast he was something of a recluse, some might say an oddball or, less kindly, a crank (Kanigel 2005).

Brandeis thought deeply about the best ways to promote what he saw as good management. For example, he wrote to Edward Filene that: "It seems to me that the time has now come when the results of the Filene experiment in cooperation and industrial democracy ought to be brought to the attention of the country" and that a "thoughtful magazine, like *McClure's*, or the *World's Work*, or the *Review of Reviews*, would be glad of the opportunity of having the subject worked up into an article" (letter from Brandeis to E. Filene, June 25, 1906). And in 1911, during the commencement speech at Brown University, described in the previous chapter, Brandeis (1914b) urged students to see business management as a profession rather than a technical subject, and an excellent career choice because of this.

"The peculiar characteristics of a profession as distinguished from other occupations, I take to be these", he went on to explain in his speech:

> *First.* A profession is an occupation for which the necessary preliminary training is intellectual in character, involving knowledge and to some extent learning, as distinguished from mere skill.
>
> *Second.* It is an occupation which is pursued largely for others and not merely for one's self.
>
> *Third.* It is an occupation in which the amount of financial return is not the accepted measure of success.
>
> Is not each of these characteristics found today in business worthily pursued?…
>
> Under these new conditions, success in business must mean something very different from mere money-making.

Later in the address, Brandeis connected these professional principles to the two exemplary case studies, of McElwain and the Filene brothers' worthy pursuits:

> McElwain and the Filenes are of course exceptional men; but there are in America to-day many with like perception and like spirit. The paths broken by such pioneers will become the peopled highways. Their exceptional methods will become accepted methods. Then the term 'Big business' will lose its sinister meaning, and will take on a new significance. 'Big business' will then mean business big not in bulk or power, but great in service and grand in manner. 'Big business' will mean professionalized business, as distinguished from the occupation of petty trafficking or mere moneymaking.

With this view and these exemplars in mind, Brandeis was hopeful that: "as the profession of business develops, the great industrial and social problems expressed in the present social unrest will one by one find solution".

But things did not work out that way. One hundred years later, Rakesh Khurana, JC Spender and others (e.g., Khurana 2007; Spender 2007; Khurana and Spender 2012) would seek to redirect the path that Management took in the twentieth century and refound it on the kind professional footing that Brandeis promoted, utilizing the rethinking of history and drawing unfavourable parallels between the path Management had taken and the development of Medicine, Law, Architecture and the Arts. Unfortunately, they do not trace a line from their present concerns to Brandeis.

Khurana's (2007) extensive history, *From Higher Aims to Hired Hands*, briefly mentions Brandeis's involvement with the Progressive movement, his development of the Brandeis Brief as a new approach to knowledge, and his advocacy of Taylor's ideas. But he neglects to mention that Brandeis made points similar to those made in his treatise a century later. This is not a criticism. How could it be? Management scholars are just not aware of Brandeis. But seeing the links now, we argue that Brandeis's ideas are a very good site to claim as the origin of Management and found future attempts to establish the subject on a new and better footing.

What our counter-history in the previous chapter revealed, is that Taylor's advantages over Brandeis (e.g., fragments of Taylor's past were much more useful to the historical narrative emerging after 1915) were such that he would be the 'site of truth' from which the chain of progress would be determined (to paraphrase Foucault). Taylor was thus anointed 'the father' of Management; and his star would rise while Brandeis's faded:

- By 1915 Taylor was dead and his legacy malleable—enabling the likes of Gantt, Kendall and Valentine, to steer Scientific Management in more 'big-business friendly' directions;
- Relatedly, those who in Dewey's words were "in control of industry — those who supply its aims", found Taylor a useful foundation and would make him "a folk hero" (Wiebe 1967: 294); whereas Brandeis, 'the American most hated by big business', was a less welcome companion;
- Third, as time went by, Taylor offered a foundation that was both a breakthrough—a discontinuity from past amateur attempts at management—and an image of a simplistic thinker that others since have built upon as Management's evolution has advanced to present heights; many of Brandeis's ideas seem advanced even today, which

is uncomfortable for anybody that would prefer to appraise their present being as better than their past (Wilson and Ross 2001; Osborn et al. 2020).

Having revealed the advantages that helped Taylor become established as the subject's founder, and having thought differently about this history to make the case for Louis Brandeis as an alternative origin or site of truth, the next two parts of this chapter sketch out 'A New History of (Sustainable) Management'. The first part on elements prior to Brandeis that looking back through the prism of his work enables us to pick out as precedents; the second from Brandeis to the present and towards a future where this history can guide us to see sustainability and management as one.

4.2 A New History for the Future

4.2.1 New History Part I

How selfish soever man may be supposed, there are evidently some principles in his nature, which interest him in the fortune of others.

Adam Smith, *The Theory of Moral Sentiments*. (1759)

As outlined in Chapter 1, Foucault's (1977: 160) approaches sought to undermine conventional notions of evolution and discontinuities as a way of invoking 'counter-memories'. Seeing Louis Brandeis as a founder of Management, and conservation and associated social and environmental goods as the object of the subject's inquiries, enables us to see a line of continuity from our present-day concerns, through Brandeis all the way back to the indigenous peoples who saw management and sustainability as interconnected. We could further populate this drawing of history with any number of dots, as these things can be seen to have been concerns for many thinkers and peoples. However, for the purposes of this first part of a brief new history, we'll focus on one. The one who may seem the least likely (given what we think we know about him), but given his revered status potentially the most consequential: Adam Smith.

Smith is significant here because he is a foundation stone often invoked to support the view of Management's good being economic efficiency.

The supposed centrality in his philosophy of the division of labour and the associated efficiency gains and his promotion of laissez-faire economics and self-interested homo economicus, is what Management history has alighted upon as the father of economics "showing great insight into the evolving management function"—George 1972: 54). He is invoked in this way to promote an evolution of ideas emerging to form Management as the subject which takes economic efficiency to be its object and good. And he is the most surprising because we subsequently assume, that he would support economic goods, rather than social or environmental ones, as the purpose of our endeavours.

Foucault (1977: 154) wrote that the "historical tradition aims at dissolving the singular event into an ideal continuity", whereas a counter-history "transposes the relationship ordinarily established between the eruption of an event and necessary continuity". And it is particularly useful to our inquiry at this point to disturb the idea that Management's foundations are built upon a union between the ideas of Adam Smith and the economic efficiency proponents. We can start to think differently about Smith and his ideas by exploring the juxtaposition below.

∞

> You think you are helping the economic system by your well-meaning laws and interferences. You are not. Let be. The oil of self-interest will keep the gears working in almost miraculous fashion. No one need plan. No sovereign need rule. The market will answer all things.

> The subjects of every state ought to contribute towards the support of the government, as nearly as possible, in proportion to their respective abilities; that is, in proportion to the revenue which they respectively enjoy under the protection of the state.

Which one of these quotations are Adam Smith's own words: the promotion of *laissez-faire* economics above, or the measured support for a progressive tax system imposed by the State below?

As we have outlined, in the middle of the twentieth century the establishment of Management as a university subject drew heavily on the notion that there was a bridge between it and the science of Economics. Correspondingly, Adam Smith is often listed as a management pioneer in textbooks and histories largely because of the kind of views espoused in the first quotation. Because he argued "the government should 'let alone' the mechanisms of the market" and its "invisible hand" and "advocated laissez-faire capitalism" (Wren 1972: 23, 24); because his "liberal thinking formed the basis of the laissez-faire doctrine" and he "laid great stress on the division of labour and its concomitant benefits" (George 1972: 54–55; Pollard 1965: 8ff.).

But despite it being closer to the view most have of Adam Smith now, and closer to the way that Smith is seen in Management history, nothing in the first quotation is Adam Smith's. The source of that quotation is *Economics* by Nobel Prize winner Paul A. Samuelson. Samuelson's (1980: 639) set up, the first-person narrative, and faux-archaic style leads the student to believe that this is Smith. But none of these sentences are Smith's own.

Samuelson's representation of Smith not unusual. Most Economics textbooks 'borrow heavily' from "Samuelson's pedagogy [and] tone" (Skousen 1997: 137); and Management texts follow suit. Despite this, it is the second quotation—a passage from Book V of *The Wealth of Nations* (hereafter WN)—that is actually written by Smith.[2]

So why did Smith promote higher taxes for the wealthy? In working through that it is worth starting with an understanding that Smith's view of mankind was unusual for his time. He believed (WN: I.ii) that:

> The difference of natural talents in different men is, in reality, much less than we are aware of; and the very different genius which appears to distinguish men of different professions... is not upon many occasions so much the cause, as the effect of the division of labour. The difference... between a philosopher and a common street porter, for example, seems to arise not so much from nature, as from habit, custom, and education.

While it is not easy for the State to affect habit and custom, it could tackle this inequity through investment in goods such as public education:

> The public [purse] can facilitate, can encourage, and can even impose upon almost the whole body of the people the necessity of acquiring those most essential parts of education... The Public can facilitate this acquisition by establishing in every parish or district a little school, where children may be taught.

[2] We use Sutherland's 2014 Oxford edition of *The Wealth of Nations* and Sen's 2010 Penguin Classics edition of *The Theory of Moral Sentiments*, but provide Smith's original Book and Chapter references.

And because the poorer classes have fewer resources to devote to education than the richer who benefit more from their start in life (WN: V.i, 2nd Third, Article 2):

> The education of the common people requires… in a civilised and commercial society, the attention of the Public more than that of people of some rank and fortune.

Hence, Smith's advocacy of using higher taxes to pay for social goods and institutions to protect and help people feel safe to deploy their labour as they see fit. To ensure that all can benefit fairly: particularly given the tendency for the growing division of labour to lead to inequitable outcomes.

This does not seem like the Adam Smith that is taught in Management (or Economics 101). Management textbooks alight only on the fragments of Smith that speak to his promotion of laissez-faire capitalism at the dawn of the industrial age, his promotion of economic self-interest overseen by market forces, and Smith's famous pin factory example about the benefits of the division of labour, as a precursor to Taylor. So how do we miss a broader view of Smith? That the excerpts reproduced above from WN are from Book V goes some way to explaining why.

WN is a book in five parts. Because Smith did not believe that the market, left alone, would answer all things, Book V addressed how the consequences of what has been advocated in the earlier books should be managed and the social goods that economic progress should provide for. It outlines the duties of government in a liberal commercial society, and important focusses for public expenditure. Book V is, therefore, a crucial counter-weight to the commercial freedoms advocated earlier.

As a consequence, Book V helps us make sense of WN as a work in Smith's oeuvre. Smith's overarching concern was the progress of sociability, and governments had a role to play in preserving the rules of justice, equality of opportunity and the infrastructure on which the progress of sociability ultimately depended (Phillipson 2011). But Book V is trimmed out of many modern presentations of WN. Take away this balance and it is not difficult to interpret Smith as the promoter of material self-interest above all, and economic efficiency as the end or good of Economics and Management.

The argument used to explain the absence of Book V from a recent Random 'Everyman' reprint is that "Books I-IV… contain the whole of what Smith had to say in carrying out his aim" (Raphael 1991: xxvii). Book V, the reader is assured, adds nothing of note. The 1970 Penguin edition, one of the most popular recent treatments, consists of Books 1[I] and 2[II] with Book 3[III] included only "in order to make maximum use of the available space" (Skinner 1970: 7). Why not fill that available space with Book V? Because the Penguin volume is "solely concerned with Smith's contribution to the principles of economics [and i]t would probably be agreed that the early books contain the central part of Smith's work" (Skinner 1970: 7). Hence, many who read *Wealth of Nations* from cover to cover (and very few do) do not read Smith explaining the point of it all: social goods and a more civilized community that provide more equal access to opportunity (goods very similar to those proposed by Brandeis).

Economics generally, and particularly at the time that Management sought to cantilever off its status, had cobbled together some key elements from Smith ("Laissez-Faire", "the division of labour is the good that causes progress", "the invisible hand of the market is for the greater good") and formed a historical view of itself that expanded outward from these. In part, this was enabled by leaving out the elements of Smith's work that did not fit the narrative being promoted by Economics and Management in the middle of the twentieth century. Writers noted that this was necessary as much of Smith's work was rather perplexing, but "*The Wealth of Nations* contains many brilliantly written passages" (Baumol and Blinder 1984: 48). So this is what they gathered up for student consumption.

In further outlining what Smith regarded as the purpose of his ideas, it will be useful to dispel three things people see as linking him to the promotion of economic efficiency for its own sake.

a. Smith did not preach 'Laissez-Faire' economics and was not the founder of neoliberalism

The idea that Smith's thinking formed the basis for the *laissez-faire* doctrine is muddled. The *laissez-faire* doctrine preceded Smith, who then dismissed it.

Laissez-faire et laissez passer (Let go and let pass) is a maxim attributed to Jacques Gournay (1712–1759) and associated with a group of Gournay's colleagues called the French *economistes*. While Smith knew this group's concepts well, the words *laissez-faire* (or *laisser-faire*) appear nowhere in Smith's vast body of work and correspondence.

There are two reasons for this. The first is that it is not a term that anybody writing in English used until the 1820s. But more importantly, Smith did not use the term (or equivalents) because he did not advocate it. Smith (WN Book IV.ix) in fact critiques the *economistes* ideas: the "capital error of [their] system", is it is undervaluing of the lower classes and industry and their notion of a pure 'perfect liberty' as the one-best way. For Quesnay, *laissez-faire* meant that government should, after a revolution and tearing down of the old ways, completely 'let alone' the mechanisms of the market. This was not Smith's view. Smith believed that the *economistes'* notion of wiping the slate clean and then leaving the market to work things out, lacked an understanding of human nature and the importance of pursuing policies that improved a country's institutions (Phillipson 2011).

Despite this key difference between Smith and his predecessors, Management and Economic histories see Smith as part of an evolutionary continuum from Quesnay through to the *laissez-faire* boosters that followed (Wren 1972: 23). Smith is further corralled into this line up by posthumously being regarded as a founding father of liberal and neoliberal schools. Steiger and Roy's (2010: 3) book *Neo-liberalism* captures this widely held (but mistaken) view:

> Classical liberals' like Adam Smith and David Ricardo preached the virtues of the 'free market' and 'laissez faire' economics. Smith is credited with creating the Scottish Enlightenment image of homo economicus – the view that people are isolated individuals whose actions reflect mostly their material self-interests. According to this view, economic and political matters are largely separable with economics claiming a superior status.

Furthermore, given that some textbooks claim that "Capitalism is sometimes called laissez faire" (McEachern 2011: 42), Smith's supposed promotion of *laissez-faire* leads many to assume he was also a preacher for the freedoms of big business and right-wing politics more generally. But despite now being a hero to many conservatives, Smith disliked party politics and factionalism of any kind and expressed no political allegiances (Buchan 2006). His strongest convictions may have been his concern for the poorest in society (e.g., WN: I.iix, V.i), and his conception that "no society can be flourishing or happy, of which the far greater part of the members are poor and miserable" (WN: I.vii). This was an idea mocked by later economists. Malthus (2013), for example, was derisory; claiming that Smith confounded the 'wealth of a state' with the "happiness of the lower classes of the people".

b. Smith did not promote the 'invisible hand of the market' and 'self-interest'

Secondly, we need to acknowledge that unlike *laissez-faire*, Smith did write 'invisible hand'. But he did not invent the phrase (one commentator notes that Moll Flanders—or at least her maker Daniel Defoe—may have a better claim seeing as Moll used the phrase in 1722—Buchan 2006). And Smith only used it three times in all his writing.

Smith refers to the invisible hand in the paper *The History of Astronomy* (c.1758), where he writes of the invisible hand to which people refer to explain natural phenomena otherwise unexplainable. Thus, it is in no way a commercial mechanism, but a circumlocution for God. He uses it a second time in his first book *The Theory of Moral Sentiments* (TMS: IV.i.10), again seeming to refer to an invisible mover, a deity, or what would have been seen in these times as the efficient (i.e., effective) cause. And, then he uses it, just once, in WN (IV.ii.9): "by directing that industry in such a manner as its produce may be of the greatest value, he intends only his own gain, and he is in this, as in many other cases, led by an invisible hand to promote an end which was no part of his intention".

Here too he may be referring to a deity or higher power. He does not explicitly link the invisible hand to the market. But the following interpretation of what Smith said from a prominent textbook is a good example of how his use of the invisible hand has come to be regarded: "According to Adam Smith, market forces allocate resources as if by an 'invisible hand' – an unseen force that harnesses the pursuit of self-interest… According to Smith, although each individual pursues his or her self-interest, the 'invisible hand' of market forces promotes the general welfare" (McEachern 2011: 42—his italics).

What has happened between Smith's writing and our understanding now is that two distinct pieces of the WN have been joined by later interpreters into "the phrase that caught the imagination of economists and business people in the twentieth century" (Buchan 2006: 26). These are the notion of the 'invisible hand', and the notion of 'self-interest'. Weaved into one they inform economists and Management students, with the gravitas of Adam Smith, that pursuing self-interest is completely justifiable, because acting according to self-interest enables the invisible hand of the market to sort things out for the best.

But this interpretation is only made possible by twisting Smith's words. Smith did not use the term self-interest. He used the term 'self-love' instead—in this one paragraph (WN Book I.ii): "He will be more likely to prevail if he can interest [others'] self-love in his favour, and show them that it is for their own advantage to do for him what he requires of them... [Thus, we should] address ourselves, not to [others'] humanity but to their self-love". Later interpreters would take self-love to be self-interest, and then take self-interest to be an immutable foundation (e.g., Stigler's characterization of WN as "a stupendous palace erected on the granite of self-interest" [1971: 265]); leading to a far more materialistic interpretation of Economics and Management than Smith intended.

The best way to understand what has been lost here is to consider the development of the French translation of WN. In all French translations prior to Garnier's (which was published in 1802), Smith's self-love was translated as amour-propre. This was how the term had always been translated when the French read the works of Hobbes, Mandeville, Butler and Hume; and amour-propre in the works of Pascal, Voltaire and Rousseau was translated as self-love in English (Force 2003). Amour-propre meant pride (and has increasingly come to mean vanity) but it also means self-regard, self-respect and self-awareness. Garnier changed the conventional translation from amour-propre to interet personnel (self-interest) in response to a moral debate of the day.

It was seen to be a paradox that self-love (a vice when interpreted as selfishness) could be the cause of virtue. Writers like Mandeville had no problem with the paradox and were happy to promote self-love as both a vice and the cause of all human action and development in his widely read Fable of the Bees.

Smith and his mentors, Hutcheson and Hume, took a different view, however. Indeed, Smith's *Theory of Moral Sentiments* (TMS, I.i.1) begins by refuting what Hume termed this 'selfish hypothesis': "How selfish soever man may be supposed, there are evidently some principles in his nature, which interest him in the fortune of others...". TMS's moral system shows how human actions are driven by self-love and a corresponding sympathy for other beings, and that the ability to put ourselves in others' shoes was a key element of our self-awareness or self-regard. This, in Smith's view, was how society progresses.

Debate between this view and the selfish hypothesis was prevalent in the last decades of the eighteenth century, and amour-propre became a hotly contested term. In *De l'Espirit*, in a chapter entitled 'On the

Abuse of Words', Claude-Adrien Helvetius argued that people increasingly mistook self-love to mean pride and vanity and thereby to be a vice. Others thought the term had been corrupted by moral and religious connotations. Helvetius' solution to the confusion was a drastic one. He dispenses with the term and promotes an alternative with less baggage: interet personnel.

Garnier's translation is in line with this new idea. And, moreover, Garnier also translates 'invisible hand' from WN (IV.ii) in a way that makes this seem more connected to Smith's 'first principle' than it was in the original. He translates "he intends only his own gain" as tout en ne cherchant que son interest personnel. Thus both 'self-love' and 'own gain' are made one in translation: Self-interest (i.e., selfishness), promotes the division of labour but this is made good for all by the market's invisible hand. Notions of self-regard as to one's role in society, and sympathy for others, are a long way from this view.

While it was a controversial break from the norm in Garnier's own time (Desrenaudes 1802), Garnier's interpretation found favour (it remained the standard French edition until 1995) and subsequent translations followed suit (Force 2003). And a similar thing happened in the English-speaking world as more serious specialized economists who saw their field as separate from (and superior to) political and moral concerns, found self-love an ill-fitting term and moved towards the more understandable (to them) idea of self-interest.

The focus on self-interest that is threaded back into WN makes it difficult for readers today to square with Smith's first book which laid out the broader ambitions of his work. Indeed, *The Theory of Moral Sentiments* (hereafter TMS) put a stake in the ground with its first sentence, quoted earlier. It is worth repeating:

> How selfish soever man may be supposed, there are evidently some principles in his nature, which interest him in the fortunes of others, and render their happiness necessary to him, though he derives nothing from it, except the pleasure of seeing it.

In other words, Smith asks, if left to their own devices, why are people not more selfish? Why are they inclined to sociability instead? TMS proceeds to provide Smith's answer: through our desire as humans to be sympathetic and share sentiments.

Smith delves into this. Given that we cannot know another's feelings directly how do we share? We can only access others' sentiments through imagining what they are experiencing by our sensory perception of how they feel: be it joy or pain or the decisions they are facing. We achieve this by looking into ourself, in other words (TMS: I.i.29): "I judge of your sight by my sight, of your ear by my ear, of your reason by my reason, of your resentment by my resentment, of your love by my love. I neither have, nor can have, any other way of judging about them". Other people do the same and we achieve mutual enrichment in this process.

How does this help us to become moral beings? Through the self-aware social practice of this simultaneous outward- and inward-looking sympathy and judgement we develop in our imagination a kind 'impartial observer' viewing and judging the conduct of others and helping us choose virtuous courses of action. This impartial observer is not our conscience; it is not guilt; nor is it just the voice of God. It is driven by our sense of wanting to be understood as sociably virtuous and wanting to concur with others we admire. Hence, Smith argued: "Man naturally desires, not only to be loved, but to be lovely: or to be that thing which is [judged by other's impartial observers] the natural and prover object of love. He naturally dreads, not only to be hated, but to be hateful; or to be that thing which is [judged] the natural and proper object of hatred" (TMS: III.i.8). These views help us understand Smith's description of the importance of self-love in the second chapter of WN.

Thus, Smith thought we actively and freely seek society for its own sake. While we may, in so doing, move further away from what Rousseau would see as our natural 'noble savage' beings, we do not do it out of insecurity or weakness or vanity, but because it helps us be better and we want to be better. And through interaction with others and learning to "humble the arrogance of [our] self-love, and [moderate] it to something that other men can go along with", we are on the path towards a virtuous life (TMS: II.ii.11). This social-civilizing process makes us the persons we would like to be and improves society overall. And this freely given, freely sought and freely moderated mutual sympathy (rather than rulers, regulations, codes or stipulations), drives the progress of the social goods of citizenship, community and civilization.

The Wealth of Nations was not the project that Smith had envisaged after TMS, or the project he envisaged as his last (his dying words were reported to be: "But I meant to have done more"), but he embraced it because focusing on political economy enabled him to show tangibly how sympathy for others and socialization could make the world a mutually better place, materially as well as socially and morally. WN would help assuage critics of TMS who thought it a nice idea but without evidence and of little material consequence. The division of labour and the material progress that this can bring was the best evidence that liberal sociable exchange is not only valuable in itself: it explains the progress of civilization. Socialization, along with self-regard and sympathy, created the trust necessary to enable the division of labour and the natural human propensity for 'truck and barter'. The division of labour developed because humans are cooperative beings who sympathize with and therefore value the endeavours of one another and will, by and large, exchange fairly if they can do so freely.

Smith thought that clumsy governments and colluding business interests that may work against this progress should be opposed. He skewers the way in which merchants—"those who were supposed to understand trade" but really only "knew perfectly how [current practices] enriched themselves"—promoted the status quo to parliaments, nobles and princes "who were conscious to themselves that they knew nothing about the matter" (WN: IV.i). Smith's notions about how big business and big government must be managed to prevent them from impinging upon citizens' freedom to innovate and advance themselves is again resonant of Brandeis's ideas.

c. The 'division of labour' is not Smith's main contribution or a central idea

There can be no doubt that Smith puts the division of labour up front in WN: it is right there in Book I. But does this mean that it is central to his philosophy?

The first thing to note in this regard is that the promotion of the division of labour was not new. Many of Smith's predecessors, like Petty, Mandeville and Hume recognized that it and specialization increased productivity. Even Plato (see The Republic, 370) understood its economic advantages (Sowell 2006).

Secondly, the presentation of the division of labour at the beginning of WN is more the result of a structural quirk than a testament to the primacy of specialization in Smith's system. As we have already seen, Smith saw the division of labour as a result of the principle of self-love, and the proper functioning of self-love is the result of other ideas Smith had advanced in the TMS: sympathy, social self-awareness and what Smith calls 'fellow-feeling'.

Some have suggested that this unscientific back-to-front presentation of evidence ahead of a theory is a practice unique to Smith's time (Buchan 2006). But Smith's structural choices can be better understood by also considering what happened with the production of TMS. Smith was not writing as a researcher would today: by converting years of work into a book that would have an appeal broader than those familiar with his specialist subjects. In developing *The Theory of Moral Sentiments*, this meant presenting his ideas in the light of Mandeville's 'selfish hypothesis', which was being widely discussed in his day, and Rousseau's recent response against this view, which was brilliant but in Smith's mind partly misguided.

WN was also a complex book: more than a pamphlet propounding the division of labour as an economic device or a management tool. As his academic peers realized, Smith's political economy was deeply embedded in a system of moral philosophy, jurisprudence and politics. But the additional readership Smith sought to reach with WN knew nothing of this. As Phillipson (2011: 217) notes: "The question was, how much of it did they need to know to make sense of his political economy. The answer was not much. So [Smith] made no formal attempt to explain [it]".

Indeed, when the WN is viewed in the context of the preparatory work laid down in his lectures at the University of Glasgow, where he preceded the technical matters relating to the division of labour with discussions on "the natural wants and demands of mankind" and their consequences for the progress of civilization, these broader discussions seem "conspicuously omitted" from *The Wealth of Nations* (Phillipson 2011: 271). But editorial choices, as with any book, had to be made and Smith started with the division of labour example, rather than the philosophy that it was an illustrative example of.

Thirdly, Smith was no blind advocate of the division of labour. While one might not see this if they only pick up on fragments of Smith's work, he seemed convinced that the division of labour created specialized idiots. Men are described by Smith (in Book V) as "mutilated and deformed in their faculties" by making "the 17th part of a pin or the 80th part of a button" (WN: V.i, 2nd Third, Article 2). These are hardly the words of a supporter. So, while the WN begins with examples of the division of labour, it is not that Smith is saying that the division of labour is good in itself: rather, he means that if we regard self-love and sociability as valuable ends, then the division of labour and the related increase in social exchange that specialization necessitates is material evidence that sociability is good, both morally and economically, as it drives the progress of civilization and citizenship.

∞

Smith's ideas, like the notions that market economics require good management to ensure that all citizens may benefit from greater opportunity; that self-regard (or self-love) helps us invoke the sentiment that promotes sympathy and, in turn, greater socialization and community; and that the division of labour is a good material example of the benefits of the mutual trust that this sympathy engenders; are built on the work of his great mentors Hutchenson and Hume. In this way, Smith's project linked to the broader aims of the Scottish Enlightenment: distilling optimistic theories of sociability that explained the progress of civilization in the light of an increasing debate around liberalism. Fundamentally, Smith was an optimist about the human condition. Thus he examined the moral, social and material progress of humanity as opposed to "the lamentable stories of the follies of so many of its rulers" which so many before him, including the economistes, had focussed upon (Phillipson 2011: 237). Together, his two books show not only that liberal governance could work; but also, that if good management was utilized, it would encourage the development of greater goods.

It is a shame, therefore, that references to Adam Smith in Management Studies make little reference to Smith's wider work or even Book V of *The Wealth of Nations*. Not least because it is in Book V that Smith actually writes directly about 'management'—the word is used over 50 times in it (the division of labour just four times, by way of contrast). But also because it would cause pause for thought about what Smith was advocating in his work; and perhaps encourage people to read *The Theory of Moral Sentiments* and think about how it outlines the ends toward which well-managed economic progress should be aimed. For Smith, the economic goods created through the division of labour, specialization and other means to improve economic efficiency, were means by which greater social and communal goods could be achieved.

While environmentalism or conservation may not have been given much consideration in Smith's world, his overarching notions of seeking sympathy and acting on social sentiments are about developing connections with fellow beings deeper than just economic or material benefit. They are, in this respect, akin to the earliest approaches to sustainable management practiced by many indigenous peoples.

Consequently, this new history has begun in a Foucauldian way: by questioning what was considered to be an obvious discontinuity that has become part of Management's historical understanding of itself. Whereas the conventional history sees a break from pre-modern approaches to the more 'scientific' thinking of moderns like Smith and Taylor, the view we are developing here seeks to trace a line from the sustainable management practices of the indigenous people with whom we began this book, through to the 'father of economics': Adam Smith. The next part of this new history draws this thread through to what we earlier proposed as an alternative origin point for Management: Louis Brandeis and the creation of Management as a subject.

4.2.2 New History Part II

While this counter-history has explicitly targeted the view that the founding father of Management is Frederick Taylor, and to knock him off this perch, it may be more useful (and in keeping with a Foucauldian approach that sought to undermine singular points of origin) not to simply switch Taylor for Brandeis. It may be better to regard them both as founders. Moreover, it would be more in keeping with the complexities of historical genealogies, to add a third point of origin: Mary Parker Follett. Subsequently, to avoid simply replacing one patriarch with another, we nominate three 'originals' for the purpose of this new history: Brandeis, Taylor and Follett.

Lyndall Urwick, the Management historian whom we described earlier in this book, at once saved Follett from obscurity and diminished her legacy by categorizing her as following on from Taylor in Management's pantheon. If we are to incorporate her here into this new history of (Sustainable) Management, perhaps we should begin by giving her higher regard. Both chronologically and philosophically, to say that she followed and built upon Taylor is a misleading simplification.

Taylor was born in 1856, the same year as Brandeis. Follett was born just 12 years later in 1868, and was doing some of her best work at the same time as the two men's ideas about management were becoming popular. They each approached Management from a different angle. Taylor was interested in how best to organize the shop floor or workshop; Brandeis, had a particular focus on professional managers and business owners and associated good management with the principles of conservation; Follett was concerned with social organizing in communities, and how this and other forms of good management contributed to the goods of community, citizenship and democracy (O'Connor 2000). And, like Adam Smith, Follett was especially interested in the role that increased access to education could play in growing individual, social and civic well-being.

Follett was a well-known and highly regarded writer and social activist in the early decades of the twentieth century. Her first book, on the development of the leadership role played by the Speaker of the House of Representatives (Follett 1896), was published to some acclaim (Tonn 2003). She was active in advocating for and organizing adult community education, and rose to become a consultant to Theodore Roosevelt on managing not-for-profit, non-governmental and voluntary organizations (Stohr and Collins 2013). She published two further books on what she had learned about management in these fields: The New State (1918) and Creative Experience (1924). Follett became an extremely popular speaker, particularly in the United Kingdom where she was the first woman invited to address the London School of Economics. However, she became increasingly ill and unable to travel after 1929. She passed away in 1933, and then was largely forgotten.

Many suggest she was forgotten because she was a woman. While this may be the easiest explanation, as with relating Brandeis's difficulty becoming accepted in the mainstream with his being Jewish, this is not the whole story. For example, Clegg et al. (2011: 468) relate Follett not getting her due because she was: "More modest than her male colleagues". But if you read her work, she does not seem particularly modest, and by most accounts this was not the case (Tonn 2003). However, it is certainly true that Follett did not enjoy the benefits that a man with her background would have been afforded. She wanted to continue her graduate studies at Harvard, but Harvard would not admit a woman for such a programme at that time. Without a higher degree, she found an academic career blocked, so no young acolytes in schools of economics or sociology sought to stand on her shoulders or promote her legacy.

Nevertheless, a further reason for the lack of uptake of Follett's ideas on Management until recently, and the lack of traction they have gotten since then, is that her thinking did not fit into the emerging narrative of the foundations of Management and they lacked a form that would make them easily classifiable on the continuum. Follett was not associated with a single school of thought, as Taylor became with Scientific Management. Her ideas could not be so easily bent into a convenient crutch for a particular ideology like Smith or Max Weber (Cummings and Bridgman 2011). Her thinking could not be plugged into a simple three or five-step model or grid of types like later theorists such as Lewin and Maslow or Myers and Briggs. And she could not easily be filed under a subfield and thus appear in an additional chapter in management textbook beyond the management history chapter: unlike Taylor (Human Resource Management); Weber (Organization Design); or Gantt (Project Management), who could appear beyond the history chapter as shaping a subfield or whose 'techniques' or designs had been built upon (Bridgman and Cummings 2021). Because Follett's theories were inserted late and were difficult to place as a stepping stone in the accepted continuity, they took on a kind of ornamental quality for managers—to be admired but not necessarily used.

This, we believe, is due to Urwick's classification of Follett's work as after and adding to Taylor in order to show the evolution of Management, even though her work does not really fit there. So, while it is true that if it wasn't for Urwick it would have been hard for later management scholars to see Follett (Graham 1995); what gets recovered from her thinking is rather ephemeral and seems somehow out of sync (Bednarek et al. 2020). We believe that there is value in this new history in placing Follett's ideas alongside Taylor and Brandeis's as points of origin, rather than as an addendum to a previously determined continuity that starts with Taylor and runs through Elton Mayo (whom Follett is often lumped with) and on to the more modern thinkers of the twentieth century.

For example, while some claim (e.g., Clegg et al. 2011) that the first management book written by a woman was *Dynamic Administration: The Collected Papers of Mary Parker Follett* (Follett 1940), it is worth remembering that this was a collection of speeches and articles curated and annotated after Follett's death by two men. Why would we not consider Follett's earlier books as some of the first in Management? That is what they are (O'Connor 2000). If we were to do so, to view Follett as standing alongside Brandeis and Taylor as a founder, what would this new history encourage us to see as the good of Management?

Mary Parker Follett moved in similar circles to Louis Brandeis. (She was a work colleague and good friend of his wife Alice and the Brandeis's hosted Follett's 50th birthday party—Tonn 2003.) Brandeis and Follett also shared some views of what the good of management was, especially the idea that the good management of resources should enable opportunity for all people to educate and improve themselves (Rosen 2016: 196). In a lecture delivered for the Bureau of Personnel Administration titled How Must Business Management Develop in Order to Become a Profession?, she outlined how managers existed for the betterment of the wider community: "not only... are you responsible for serving your community, but... you are partly responsible for there being any community to serve". And within that community, the purpose of management was, in Follett's words: "to give an opportunity for human development through the better organization of human relationships"—an end she saw as every bit as noble as the aims of justice, health and beauty touted by more established professions of law, medicine and architecture (Follett 1940: 97–98).

Follett outlined the means by which managers might seek to achieve these ends in *The New State* and *Creative Experience*. Her two main Management ideas, or areas of theorizing, relate to how to structure organizations and management to best provide opportunities for human development; and how to manage and encourage innovation.

The view of management emerging out of the factories that were beginning to dominate the increasingly industrial landscape in Follett's America at this time, was one where managers issued plans for workers to follow without question. Follett saw good organization as a group activity involving the exchange of views, from management to workers, workers to workers and workers to management, with the aim of working towards integration the best ideas from the collective and unifying behind them: in much the same way as a good educator might work with adult students, incorporating their experiences (something that Follett knew a lot about). Often, Follett recognized, good ideas and inspiration may come not from managers higher up the hierarchy, but from those 'closer to the ground'.

This influenced Follett to articulate a view of good leadership as not just 'top-down', but as a dynamic process where relationships were more lateral. Brandeis too had advocated greater worker involvement with decision-making in this way, and held up the Filene brothers as exemplars in this regard, but Follett went deeper in theorizing why this was a better approach to management. She articulated a theory that argued for replacing a view of good managers as exercising formal 'power over' the workforce with the view that they would be more effective to think of their role as sharing 'power with' (Follett 1918).

Relatedly, Follett's ideas of mutual influence going both ways between management and workers saw the possibility for followers to affect leaders as much as leaders affect followers. As such, Follett articulated a conception of management that urged leaders to replace hierarchies with empowered group networks charged with collectively developing common purposes.

This led Follett to a second set of key insights into how managers could achieve the good of their profession. This related to the encouragement of creativity. Brandeis similarly highlighted the importance of this, noting that "the application of the principle of industrial democracy [one of Brandeis's key principles] to the reality of industrial conditions necessitated social invention". And that, as a consequence: "American legislators must be inventors. Businessmen must be inventors" (Brandeis, in Lief, 1936: 224). But whereas Brandeis had a few good 'war stories' like that of the Filene's and McElwain, Follett went on to explore and theorise how innovation could be managed effectively in far greater depth.

Follett's work experiences had led her to see conflict as healthy—not something to be managed out or supressed. To support this, she articulated the idea of 'Constructive Conflict' where creative solutions emerged from surfacing, examining and debating discordant points of view. The best approach to conflict was not to ascertain which side was right, she argued, but to share and seek to understand each perspective and integrate legitimate interests to create new solutions. This is where essential creativity, innovation and problem-solving comes from, so even if it might be difficult we should embrace it (Follett 1924).

Hence, whereas other management thinkers advocated a homogeneous workforce where, because of a strong unified culture, individuals would think in similar ways and be more efficient because of this, Follett advocated diversity in organizations and groups. She sounds very modern as we read her phrases such as "We must face life as it is and understand that diversity is its most essential feature" (Follett 1924: 300); but nearly a century ago Mary Parker Follett was outlining the benefits of things we might consider new realizations: that diversity and constructive conflict are what drives innovation and are thus the life-blood of a good organization.

∞

This is a good point at which to take stock. By way of developing a new history of Management, one with Sustainable Management at its heart, what have we got that could be put forward as a counter-history to encourage thinking differently for the future? A new history that could alternatively appear in a Management textbook, informing students of the relevant historical identity of the field and inspiring managers in the present in new ways.

Firstly, we might note that Sustainable Management was practiced in various forms by pre-modern or indigenous societies as they considered how to develop and share resources, support one another, and live in balance with their natural surroundings.

Given limited pages in which to tell this history, we might move to then consider the way in which Adam Smith, who would later be named the father of economics, couched his ideas and theories within a view of how economic progress should be understood within and aimed towards social goods. How we are, as humans, inclined toward, and should be encouraged to make manifest, sympathy for others in our environment and direct economic gains toward social and civic goods.

We might consider Smith's work to be prior to the establishment of Management as a subject (although as we have noted, Smith did have a lot to say about management—see Book V of *The Wealth of Nations*). Then, after Smith in this arrangement, we might outline three key individuals who advanced management thinking at the time when it came to be considered a serious subject of general concern, the first two decades of the twentieth century: Brandeis, Taylor and Follett.

Louis Brandeis created Management as a subject with the specific purpose of winning a legal case against a big business unfairly treating smaller businesses and individual customers. But he also connected this endeavour to a movement that he had been introduced to by Gifford Pinchot, who, along with his team, developed it as a way for Theodore Roosevelt to build an alternative view of the American Dream—one not based on absolute individual freedom to develop an enterprise, make as much money as possible and pay no heed to any collateral damage. This was the Conservation Movement. Subsequently, influenced by his thirty years of advising businesses and teaching business and law students, a practice based on a belief in employee voice and democracy, creating opportunities for all to advance themselves, and protecting and growing good citizenry and community in increasingly industrial environments, Brandeis defined the central motive, or good, of Management as conservation. If we were to include case examples in this new history, cases that might be seen as exemplars of good management, we could include those that Brandeis himself promoted about McElwain's Shoe Factory or Filene's Department Stores.

Frederick Taylor's principles of management are also foundational. It is hard to see that Brandeis's attempts to claim management as a body of knowledge that executives were negligent if they were not aware of it, would have worked if he was not able to draw on Taylor's ideas. Taylor made it his life work to develop theories of management, and while their mechanical and inflexible application seem archaic to us today, there can be no doubt that their application helped increase order and reduce the needless waste of resources at a time in history when devil-may-care industrial expansion, and pollution, and social and environmental conditions were rapidly deteriorating (they also, when applied thoughtfully, enabled employment to be less irregular). And while Taylor's primary focus was on developing tools to help managers increase economic efficiency, he linked the pursuit of this to greater goods: conservation and a greater economic resources to be shared with workers.

Whereas Brandeis approached Management from the perspective of the professions, and Taylor from the perspective of the shop floor, Mary Parker Follett approached the subject from a different background: working with social, educational and not-for-profit organizations. As factories and workshops spread to envelop cities and Taylor and Brandeis's ideas about Scientific Management were adopted by organizations, Follett's ideas about management addressed the problems with this view devolving into a generic top-down, one-best way approach to applying the subject where the senior management always knows best. While she shared Brandeis's view that management should be aimed toward improving social and civic goods, she spent the bulk of her career theorizing and developing means by which managers could contribute to the achievement of these goods. Arguing, in particular, for: multilateral dialogue and the sharing of ideas; managers not just broadcasting instructions but listening; and sharing power with rather than always exercising power over employees; and, for increasing diversity and looking at problems from multiple perspectives as a way of promoting essential innovation.

Accepting Brandeis and Follett alongside Taylor as founders may be a difficult leap for those within the field. For one thing, it goes against a history of Management that has been gradually piled up over one hundred years. We are not talking about just looking back a few decades and tweaking some aspects near the top of the mountain of knowledge depicted in Fig. 2.1 back in Chapter 2 of this book. We are promoting a history that seeks to repile the very foundations of that edifice: an extremely unsettling exercise.

Secondly, and perhaps even more of a challenge is the concession that comes with acknowledging Brandeis and Follett as founders. Seeing their ideas at that start of the enterprise forces us to accept that Management, and those practicing it—us, in other words—have not evolved or advanced as much as we might have hoped, if at all. In fact, much of what they advanced, ideas that existed in this version of the past of Sustainable Management, are disconcertingly similar to where we have struggled to arrive at here in the present. For example:

- Brandeis's work sought to highlight the corrosive nature—corrosive for individuals and of social goods—of gig working or irregular employment; something that management theorists today are beginning to grapple with.
- Similarly, Brandeis's ideas about supporting local small businesses resonate with the recent promotion of circular economies and social procurement: whereby organizations encourage trade between local enterprises as a way of achieving social, environmental and economic goods.
- Brandeis and Follett's ideas about the value of workplace democracy seem to be the opposite of what we considered Management was about 100 years ago.
- Follett's promotion of encouraging diversity as a means of increasing creativity and innovation, and managers and leaders being influenced by workers as much as the other way around, might appear to be theories that modern researchers have only recently revealed—not a century old.
- Follett's focus on researching management with groups as the unit of analysis may be ahead of our times. So much of management research conducted in business schools now employ an atomistic focus on individuals or individual organizations, largely because this kind of research is easier to do and publish efficiently using quantitative methods, and partly due to following decades of precedent and training. It would be nice to think that greater recognition of Follett's work as foundational might encourage others to see management as a group or team exercise and research it accordingly.

Subsequently, a new history like this, which sees our forebears as our intellectual equals, is challenging. But, the advantage that we gain from forgoing the pretence of intellectual evolution, is that it can make the promotion of sustainability in management foundational and fundamental to our subject, rather than a recent trend waiting to be overlaid by the next 'new thing'.

But getting back to the new history we are advancing, after outlining those three foundational figures we might pick up and expand upon the threads that are already listed as precursors to Sustainable Management and which we covered in Chapter 2: growing awareness of the environmental effects of industrial pollution from the 1960s, important books like *Silent Spring*, the growing push at the United Nations and other international organizations for greater accountability in relation to environmental and social goods as well as economic gains. Then, through the emergence of corporate reports listing achievements in regard to these goods, all the way on to the 17 Sustainable Development Goals, which are becoming increasingly cited and deployed by organizations.

However, there are additional aspects that we might learn from looking to be influenced by a new history of (Sustainable) Management, and incorporating influences beyond the line from indigenous thinking through Adam Smith and the three founders presented here. We'll address three below, relating firstly to the incorporation of a greater diversity of cultures, secondly to incorporating a broader range of case studies that combine economic and social concerns, and thirdly a questioning of the rule of the conventional 'three pillars' of sustainable development.

First, we might begin to address the fact that our new history lacks diversity, and build upon Follett's lessons, by incorporating some of the new work done on 'decolonizing' the management curriculum and developing histories of those marginalized from the historical annals that were largely white, male and European/Anglo-Saxon (Nkomo 2011; Cummings and Bridgman 2016). Most of these works promote sustainable environmental and social goods, and a focus on community engagement. For example, Prieto and Phipps's (2019) recent work on African-American management pioneers like Madame C.J. Walker and Charles Clinton Spaulding and their emphasis on developing collective, cooperative advantage rather than seeing management in terms of competitive advantage and individual financial gain, could be fruitfully woven into a new history of Sustainable Management and, indeed, Management in general.

Second, we might reflect on how indigenous peoples, and Brandeis, did not draw much if any distinction between conserving social and environmental goods: they saw them as part of the same function that needed to be balanced with economic resource development. It is interesting, in this regard, to reflect on how what has come to be seen as the "Three Pillars of Sustainable Development" (see Fig. 2.2 in Chapter 2) divide the three into columns, and how perhaps the most impactful examples of promoting Sustainability have combined environmental *and* social concerns in concert against the forces for economic efficiency gains. While the reports of Sustainable Management's development in textbooks tend to focus on big government, and NGO projects like the development of the 'Our Common Future' report and the Sustainable Development Goals, and the wonders of large modern corporations like Google, perhaps other cases would prove more compelling? For example, looking at how the Bhopal and Chernobyl tragedies brought together and galvanized activists against the degradation of human *and* environmental goods could encourage us to bring cases like this into our curriculum. In the case of Chernobyl, many argue that the forces it unleashed led to the downfall of one modernity's two great political systems (Dawson 1996; Marples 1991; Plokhy 2018).

The *third* addition we might incorporate into thinking different about Sustainable Management as a result of our new history, addresses the 'second thoughts' of Triple Bottom Line creator John Elkington described in Chapter 2. This is that we might look again at whether the framework that we promote for implementing Sustainable Management needs to be arranged, as it currently is, in three pillars? When sustainable development is organized into three categories, particularly with economic goods positioned first, each of the other two may appear lesser than it. It might be interesting to reflect on how Brandeis's and Adam Smith's views of management placed the achievement of social and/or environmental goods as *ends* and increasing economic efficiency as the *means* by which these ends could be achieved.

Relatedly, recent developments in management in indigenous communities have developed the Triple Bottom Line framework into a Quadruple Bottom line, where culture is the additional category and the conventional three bottom lines are wrapped into promoting a greater good of sustaining, developing and passing on a thriving culture for future generations (Harmsworth et al. 2002). And, in working with and being advised by Māori organizations recently, we have sought to weave in a fifth bottom line: political representation (www.tematarau.co.nz or look for the 'Ruruku Strategy Canvas' on youtube). Here, the thinking is that without achieving significant political gains in developing cultural, social, environmental and economic goods, indigenous groups will be unable to secure the necessary voice, or seats at the table, to ensure that they can control their own sustainable development for the future.

In light of these recognitions, it may be that our new history could provide pause for thought as to whether it is best to see three pillars of sustainable development; and whether it is best, in such an arrange-ment, to see the economic pillar as the first foundation with others at later appendages. Perhaps it may be better to view just two sides to be balanced: social/environmental goods with economic goods; or to see economic development to be an end to greater social, environmental, civic or cultural goods. We might, on this train of thought, also ponder whether the 17 SDGs usefully capture all possibilities, or dilutes our efforts by enumerating so many categories that people will struggle to remember and enact them all (see Fig. 4.2).

Fig. 4.2 The United Nation's Sustainable Development Goals. Reproduced with permission

Whatever a new history of Sustainable Management like the one we have begun to sketch out here might include, it is clear that by seeing continuity from pre-modern approaches to today (rather than seeing these as other than modern Management), by viewing Adam Smith in a more rounded fashion, and by seeing not just Taylor, but also Brandeis and Follett as founders, origins and 'sites of truth', this history could also be seen as a history of Management more generally. And in so doing, this kind of innovation with regard to sustainability can be seen as one with, rather than an add-on to, Management.

What the creation of the counter-history in this book has sought to do, is to show that it is possible to rethink the foundations and fundamental elements of Management; to see, as Foucault expressed, that the goods towards which we aim our endeavours are not God-given or objectively independent of us. They are invented by us, and then defined over time by our practices. In this spirit, we can redefine the history of Management as one with Sustainable Management at its core. This can encourage us to manage otherwise from how we have conventionally done for the last 100 years: where we may have practiced our profession with the assumption that economic efficiency was our object and gave rise to our subject, and was both our animating good and our means for achieving that good. In short, if we are to think differently about Management in the present and the future, a good place to start would be by turning back and looking again, and looking differently, at our past.

4.3 About-Face

We concluded Chapter 2 by describing how some have argued that the best way to advance Sustainable Management is to face the future with a clear head and new mindsets. But this book ends by promoting an alternative outlook. A recommendation to advance by turning back, looking again and thinking differently about the relationship between management and sustainability that conventional historical views promote.

After Chapter 2, we applied the approaches of Michel Foucault to create a counter-history. This critiqued the conventional history of management and the foundations, origins, the continuities, the discontinuities, and the good that history promotes as a means of "getting free of oneself". This phrase speaks to the importance of rethinking a body or an institution's history in order to approach the future in a different way, without the conventional baggage.

The conventional understanding is that the subject of Management arose hand-in-hand with the advance of industrialization, its founder was Frederick Taylor, and its fundamental good economic efficiency. This was a formation that made sense for those seeking to promote the subject and write its history in the middle decades of the twentieth century.

Our counter-history looked behind this, identifying Louis Brandeis as promoting Management in a different way at the outset. Brandeis and those he worked with saw Management as a part of a movement for environmental and social goods, the preservation of which had been made a problem by the rapid advance of industrialization and *laissez faire* capitalism in the United States at the turn of the twentieth century. Brandeis defined the field's 'central motive', its good, its object, as conservation. But Brandeis was not a founder, and this was not a good, that resonated with those who promoted and practiced management and wrote its history in the decades that followed.

Beyond this, in place of the discontinuities promoted by the historical evolution drawn from Management's 'point of origin', our counter-history identified continuities; and instead of assumed continuities it surfaced discontinuities. Among other reversals in this regard, our counter-history promoted the following:

- Whereas we might think Sustainable Management a break with the past, a clever new approach that only we today can get our heads around; our counter-historical thinking enables us to draw a continuous line from pre-modernity to the present.
- Whereas we might consider economic efficiency and its management to be a consistent, universal, over-arching good; we utilized a juxtaposition of quotations to begin to unpick this idea, and countered that economic efficiency—in itself and as the object or good of management—was a modern creation only elevated from a means to achieve other ends to an end in itself around the second decade of the twentieth century.
- Whereas we may have thought of Management as a continuous evolution from Frederick Taylor's point of origin, where truths build upon one another to create a rising mountain of knowledge; we saw a schism where Management was about social and environmental goods, and then it wasn't, as Scientific Management moved in another direction. And we argue that after this twentieth century

blip where we saw economic efficiency as fundamental, we may return to seeing other goods as Management's reason for being.

- And, whereas we might have come to see economic and social and environmental goods as discrete and covering all there is, we have suggested that they may be one. Or that they might be added to, depending upon the goods that communities may identify as important to them, thereby rethinking the primary framework that Management uses to express Sustainable Management: the Triple Bottom Line.

If the new history we outlined in this chapter were to become the accepted history of Management: where we could trace a line from indigenous societies to Adam Smith's *Theory of Moral Sentiments*, to Brandeis, Taylor, and Follett, and on to the present day through additional foundational thinkers like those identified in Prieto and Phipps and other's research, Charles Clinton Spaulding and Madame C.J. Walker, for example; to talk now of Sustainable Management as being different from 'normal' Management would make no sense. They would be one and the same. The modern subject of Management would be a continuity of the pre-modern approaches described in Chapter 1. It would have sustainability at heart; and we would not see sustainability as a discontinuity, a novelty, a trend, a prefix to be added to quell the fallout, like a silencer added to the end of a gun.

Whatever the accepted end or good of a subject may be, there can be little argument that it provides a focal point, a 'north star' to guide progress, a line of sight from the past to the present to the future: an end that influences what we choose as our aim in practice or the dependent variables in our research. Either explicitly or implicitly, as our actions in these arenas become embedded, we are increasingly channelled by the goods we associate progress with.

Recognizing this, Jeffrey Pfeffer (2016: 666) has argued that if we are to think differently in management, "understanding the predominance of performance, productivity, and efficiency as the dependent variables of most interest, should be a prime research priority". Others have suggested the need for "more detailed genealogical charts" that show the incremental development of what we see as Management's aims (Bodrožić and Adler 2017: 115). And Walsh et al's. (2003: 559) work has found that despite founding documents related to the Academy of Management in the late 1950s, which promoted both economic and social objectives, "our field has pursued society's economic objectives much more".

We argue that one of the causes of this—a cause that goes unrecognized—is our historical understanding of management, as a subject and as a practice: an understanding that became hard-baked in latter decades of the twentieth century and has not been revisited since; and our understanding of Sustainable Management in relation to that as a later 'add-on'.

On first view, we might think that the problem is that we have put the cart before the horse, seeing economic goods as ahead of others. But really we have put another cart before the cart—we've come to accept as an immutable fact that economic efficiency is both the foundational end *and* the means that defines Management. While we may have made the wheels turn more efficiently in this way, it is little wonder that the progress of this vehicle has been disappointing. However, with a growing appreciation that what we regard as the 'goods' we are aiming to achieve comes through innovation—to return to Foucault's words with which we began this chapter—we may be encouraged to think again and think differently. Just as those in the middle decades of the twentieth century invented economic efficiency as the good guiding their endeavours, we may look back now and invent a new North Star to guide us. By turning back, we can see, and we can make, sustainability the fundamental good that guides everything we manage.

References

Baumol, W.J., and A.S. Blinder 1984. *Economics: Principles and policy*, 2nd ed. New York: Harcourt Brace Jovanovich.

Bednarek, R., S. Cummings, & T. Bridgman. 2020. Out of place: management studies' temporal misplacements of Mary Parker Follett. *Academy of Management Proceedings* (Vol. 2020, No. 1, p. 16471).

Bodrožić, Z., and P. Adler. 2017. The evolution of management models: A neo-Schumpeterian theory. *Administrative Science Quarterly* 63 (1): 85–129.

Brandeis, L.D. 1911. *Scientific management and the railroads*. New York: Engineering.

Brandeis, L.D. 1914a. Other people's money and how the bankers use it. *Harper's*.

Brandeis, L.D. 1914b. *Business: A profession*. New York: Small, Maynard & Co.

Bridgman, T., and S. Cummings. 2021. *A very short, fairly interesting and reasonably cheap book about management theory*. London: Sage.

Buchan, J. 2006. *Adam Smith and the pursuit of perfect liberty*. London: Profile Books.

Clegg, S.R., M. Kornberger, and T. Pitsis. 2011. *Managing and organizations: An introduction to theory and practice*. London: Sage.

Cummings, S., and T. Bridgman. 2011. The relevant past: Why the history of management should be critical for our future. *Academy of Management Learning and Education* 10: 77–93.

Cummings, S., and T. Bridgman. 2016. The limits and possibilities of history: How a wider, deeper and more engaged understanding of business history can foster innovative thinking. *Academy of Management Learning and Education* 15 (2): 1–18.

Dawson, J.I. 1996. *Eco-nationalism, anti-nuclear activism and national identity in Russia*. Lithuania and Ukraine: University of North Carolina Press.

Desrenaudes, M.B. 1802. Review of Garnier's *The Wealth of Nations*. *La décade philosophique, littéraire and politique*, (vol. 36).

Dewey, J. 1916. *Democracy and education: An introduction to the philosophy of education*. New York: Macmillan.

Follett, M.P. 1896. *The Speaker of the House of Representatives*. Green: Longmans.

Follett, M.P. 1918. *The new state*. Green: Longmans.

Follett, M.P. 1924. *Creative experience*. Green: Longmans.

Follett, M.P. 1940. *Dynamic administration: The collected papers of Mary Parker Follett*, ed. H. Metcalf and L. Urwick. Pitman: London.

Force, P. 2003. *Self-interest before Adam Smith: A genealogy of economic science*. Cambridge University Press.

Foucault, M. 1977. *Language, counter-memory, practice*. Ithaca, NY: Cornell University.

Foucault, M. 1988. An interview with Michel Foucault conducted by Michael Bess, San Francisco. *History of the Present* 4 (Spring 1988): 1–13.

Gantt, H. 1911. *Work, wages, and profits: Their influence on the cost of living*. Engineering Magazine: New York.

George, C.S. 1968/1972. *The history of management thought*, 1st/2nd editions. Englewood Cliffs, NJ: Prentice Hall.

Graham, P. 1995. *Mary Parker Follett–Prophet of management: A celebration of writings from the 1920s*. Brighton: Harvard Business School Press.

Haber, S. 1964. *Efficiency and uplift: Scientific management in the progressive era 1890–1920*. Chicago: University of Chicago Press.

Harmsworth, G., K. Barclay-Kerr, and T.M. Reedy. 2002. Maori sustainable development in the 21st century: The importance of Maori values, strategic planning and information systems. *He Puna Korero: Journal of Maori and Pacific Development* 3 (2): 40.

Kakar, S. 1970. *Frederick Taylor: A study in personality and innovation*. MIT Press.

Kanigel, R. 2005. *The one best way: Frederick Winslow Taylor and the enigma of efficiency*. New York: Viking.

Kavanagh, D. 2013. Problematizing practice: MacIntyre and management. *Organization* 20 (1): 103–115.

Khurana, R. 2007. *From higher aims to hired hands; The social transformation of American business schools and the unfulfilled promise of management as a profession*. Princeton, NJ: Princeton University Press.

Khurana, R., and J. C. Spender. (2012). Herbert A. Simon on what ails business schools: More than 'a problem in organizational design'. *Journal of Management Studies* 49 (3): 619–639.

Knoll, M. 2009. From Kidd to Dewey: the origin and meaning of 'social efficiency'. *Journal of Curriculum Studies* 41 (3): 361–391.

Lief, A. 1936. *Brandeis: The personal history of an American ideal*. Pittsburg, PA: Telegraph.

MacIntyre, A.C. 1984. *After virtue*. Notre Dame: University of Notre Dame Press.

Malthus, T. 2013. *An essay on the principle of population* (first published 1798). New Haven, CT: Yale University Press.

Marples, D.R. 1991. *Ukraine under Perestroika: Ecology, economics and the Workers' Revolt*. New York:

McEachern, W.A. 2011. *Economics: A contemporary introduction*, 9th ed. Boston, MA: Cengage Learning.

Nkomo, S.M. 2011. A postcolonial and anti-colonial reading of 'African' leadership and management in organization studies: Tensions, contradictions and possibilities. *Organization* 18 (3): 365–386.

O'Connor, E.S. 2000. Integrating Follett: History, philosophy and management. *Journal of Management History* 6 (4): 167–190.

Osborn, H., K.D. Markman, and J.L. Howell. 2020. Nostalgia and temporal self-appraisal: Divergent evaluations of past and present selves. *Self and Identity*: 1-22.

Pfeffer, J. 2016. Why the assholes are winning: Money trumps all. *Journal of Management Studies* 53 (4): 663–669.

Phillipson, N. 2011. *Adam Smith: An enlightened life*. London: Penguin.

Plokhy, S. 2018. *Chernobyl: History of a tragedy*. Penguin UK.

Polakov, W.N. 1922. The measurement of human work. In *The Gantt chart, a working tool of management*, ed. W. Clark. New York: Ronald Press.

Pollard, S. 1965. *The genesis of modern management: A study of the industrial revolution in Great Britain*. Cambridge: Harvard University Press.

Prieto, L.C., and S.T. Phipps. 2019. *African American management history: Insights on gaining a cooperative advantage*. Bingly: Emerald.

Raphael, D.D. 1991. *The wealth of nations*. London: Random.

Rosen, J. 2016. *Louis D. Brandeis: American prophet*. London: Yale University Press.

Samuelson, P.A. 1980. Economics, 10th ed. New York: McGraw-Hill.

Skinner, A. 1970. *The wealth of nations*. Harmondsworth: Penguin.

Spender, J.C. 2007. Management as a regulated profession: An essay. *Journal of Management Inquiry* 16 (1): 32–42.

Skousen, M. (1997). The perseverance of Paul Samuelson's economics. *Journal of Economic Perspectives* 11(2): 137–152.

Steiger, M.B., and R.K. Roy. 2010. *Neo-liberalism: A very short introduction*. Oxford: Oxford University Press.

Stigler, G.J. 1971. Smith's travels on the ship of state. *History of Political Economy* 3 (2): 265–277.

Stohr, M., and P.A. Collins. 2013. *Criminal justice management: Theory and practice in justice-centered organizations*. London: Routledge.

Sowell, T. 2006. *On classical economics*. New Haven, CT: Yale University Press.

Tonn, J.C. 2003. *Mary P. Follett: Creating democracy, transforming management*. New Haven, CT: Yale University Press.

Urofsky, M.I. 1981. *Louis D. Brandeis and the progressive tradition*. Boston, MA: Little, Brown.

Walsh, J.P., K. Weber, and J.D. Margolis. 2003. Social issues and management: Our lost cause found. *Journal of Management* 29 (6): 859–881.

Wiebe, R.H. 1967. The search for order, 1877–1920. New York: Macmillan.

Wilson, A.E., and M. Ross. 2001. From chump to champ: people's appraisals of their earlier and present selves. *Journal of Personality and Social Psychology* 80 (4): 572.

Wrege, C., and A. Perroni. 1974. Taylor's pig tale: A historical analysis of Frederick W. Taylor's pig-iron experiments. *Academy of Management Journal* 17: 6–27.

Wren, D.A. 1972/1994. *The evolution of management thought*, 1st/4th ed. Ronald Press: New York.

Index

A
African American management pioneers, 135
American Association of Collegiate Schools of Business (AACSB), 23
American Dream, 50, 54, 80, 132
American Society of Mechanical Engineers (ASME), 61
Aristotle, 41, 42, 45, 46
Australia, 1–3

B
Ballinger, Richard, 54
Barnard, Chester, 23, 41, 42, 45, 46
Bhopal, 136
Big business, 40, 48–50, 54, 56, 79, 80, 84–86, 112, 119, 124
Bigness, 79
Brandeis Brief, the, 81–83, 111, 113
Brandeis, Louis D., 12, 41, 46–49, 54–64, 67–76, 78–82, 84–87, 90–95, 97–99, 106–114, 118, 124, 127–134, 136, 138
Brown University, 75, 84, 111
Brundtland Report, 30
Business—A Profession, 84, 99, 109

C
California, 2
Cannibals With Forks, 31
Carmody, Kev, 2
Carnegie, Andrew, 23–25, 50, 72, 73
Carnegie report, 25
Carson, Rachel, 33
Chandler, Alfred D., 23, 29, 95, 96, 98
Chernobyl, 136
Children's Bureau, 82
Chinese, 9, 20, 27
Circular economy, 80, 134
Citizenship, 55, 80, 99, 123, 126, 128
Classical perspective, classical school (of management), 17, 19, 20
Collier's Magazine, 54

S. Cummings and T. Bridgman, *The Past, Present and Future of Sustainable Management*,
https://doi.org/10.1007/978-3-030-71076-7

Columbia University, 47, 82
Community, 79, 80, 99, 106, 108, 118, 123, 126, 128, 130, 132, 135, 136
Congress, 50
Conservation, 3, 5, 11, 33, 34, 40, 46, 50–56, 58–60, 63, 64, 66–69, 80, 85, 90–92, 96, 98, 99, 106–108, 114, 126, 128, 132, 133
Conservation movement, 12, 48–51, 53, 66, 69, 85, 95, 98, 132
Constructive conflict, 131
Cooke, Morris, 64, 90, 91
Cooperative advantage, 135
Copely, F.B., 91
Counter-history, 7, 9–12, 16, 35, 40, 41, 46, 109, 113, 115, 127, 138
Country, 2, 3, 40, 51, 59, 63, 68, 71, 79, 80, 85, 111, 119
Covid-19, 1
Creative Experience, 128
Creativity, 131, 134
Cultural burning, 2, 3
Culture, 3, 4, 19, 131, 135, 136

D

Deleuze, Gilles, 15
Democratic Party, 85
Dewey, John, 108, 109, 113
Diocletian, 95
Diversity, 131, 133–135
Division of labour, 29, 115–118, 122, 124–126
Donut economy, 80
Drucker, Peter F., 23, 97
Drury, Howard B., 47, 56, 57, 91, 92

E

Eastern Rail Road Company, 46
Eastern Rate Case (ERC), 56, 84, 85, 94
Economics, 4, 5, 23–26, 28–31, 33, 34, 40, 43, 49, 50, 55, 56, 69, 72–74, 76, 80–82, 84, 85, 95, 97, 106, 111, 115–119, 121, 124–128, 132–137
Economistes, 118, 119, 126
Ecopornography, 33
Efficiency, 11, 12, 18, 22, 23, 26–31, 34, 40–46, 48, 49, 53, 55, 58–60, 64, 66–69, 80, 90, 91, 93, 96–99, 106–108, 114, 115, 117, 118, 126, 133, 136, 138
  economic efficiency, 12, 23, 26, 28–31, 34, 40, 41, 43–46, 67, 93, 97–99, 106–108, 114, 115, 117, 118, 126, 133, 136, 138
  social efficiency, 55, 108
Egyptians, 11, 20, 27, 96
Elkington, John, 31, 33–35, 136
Emerson, Harrington, 57, 61, 68, 91, 92
Environmentalism, 32–34, 126
Environmental Management as an Opportunity, 32
Environmental Protection Agency (EPA), 31, 33

F

Fayol, Henri, 94
Filene, Abraham L., 55
Filene, Edward A., 55, 111
Filene's Department Store, 76, 133
Fire, 1–3
First peoples, 2, 3
Follett, Mary Parker, 94, 127–135, 138
Ford report, 25

Foucault, Michel, 5–12, 15, 16, 21, 40, 41, 49, 69, 92, 98, 106, 109, 114, 115, 138

G
Galileo, 28, 93
Gantt, Henry, 57, 58, 90, 106, 113, 129
George, C.S., 29, 42, 45, 94–96, 115, 116
Gig workers, 134
Gilbreth, Frank B., 57, 58, 61, 67
Gillette Safety Razor Company, 71
Glavis, Louis, 54
Goldmark, Alice, 71
Goldmark, Josephine, 81, 82
Good, the, 16, 21, 22, 26, 27, 29, 42, 46, 77, 93, 97, 106–109, 118, 128–131, 138
Google, 29, 136
Gournay, Jacques, 118
Greenwashing, 33
Gulick, Luther H., 21, 22, 93

H
Hamel, Gary, 97
Harvard Law School, 70, 83
Hegelian, 6
Hippocrates, 22
Hippy-culture, 34
Hobbes, 121
Hoffman, A.J., 32
Homestead massacre, 72, 73
Hume, David, 121, 124, 126

I
Indigenous peoples, 2, 4, 11, 114, 126, 127, 136
Industrial democracy, 77, 90, 111, 131
Industrialization, 11, 28, 29, 40, 48, 49, 51, 56, 79, 80, 96
Innovation, 2, 6, 8, 9, 19, 28, 41, 56, 71, 81, 82, 106, 130, 131, 133, 134, 138
Insurance industry, 74
Interstate Commerce Commission (ICC), 46, 48, 59, 61, 68, 69
Invisible hand, the, 118, 120
Isaiah, 86

J
Jefferson, Thomas, 95
Jesus, 95, 96
John Hopkins University, 72
Judaism, 85

K
Kelley, Florence, 81, 82
Kelly, Paul, 2
Kendall, Henry, 90, 91, 113
Kent, Robert T., 57, 58, 61
Khurana, Rakesh, 113
Kierkegaard, Soren, 87
Klein, Naomi, 4, 5, 33
Koontz, Harold, 26, 42

L
Laissez-faire, 40, 48, 49, 84, 115–120
Langdell, Christopher Columbus, 70, 78, 81
Leadership, 20, 42, 63, 128, 130
Lerner, Max, 59, 87
Lewin, Kurt, 129
Locke, Robert, 24, 25

M
MacIntyre, Alasdair C., 107
Malthus, 119

Mandeville, 121, 124, 125
Māori, 136
Maslow, Abraham, 129
Massachusetts Institute of Technology (MIT), 72–74, 111
McElwain, William H., 75, 76, 78, 91, 92, 111, 112
McElwain's Shoe Factory, 133
McKinsey Consultants, 111
Mellen, Charles S., 58, 84
Midvale Steel Factory, 61
Millar, Minyawe, 3
Minimum wage, 77, 82
Modern, 2–5, 11, 21, 25, 29, 43, 51, 56, 72, 73, 93, 97, 98, 117, 127, 129, 131, 134, 136
Moody's Magazine, 61
Morgan, Gareth, 98
Morgan, J.P., 50
Moses, 20
Muller vs. Oregon, 81, 82
Murri, 2
Myers and Briggs, 129

N
Naisbett, John, 33
National Consumers League, 81, 82
Neo-liberalism, 118, 119
New-ageism, 34
New Deal, 86
New Freedom, 85
New Haven Railway Corporation, 84
New York Garment Workers' Strike, 55
New York Public Libraries, 82

O
Other People's Money, 84
Our Common Future, 18, 30, 136
Oxford English Dictionary (OED), 43, 45

P
Pascal, Blaise, 121
People, planet, profit, 31
Pinchot, Amos, 54, 59
Pinchot-Ballinger case, 53
Pinchot, Gifford, 50, 51, 53–55, 59, 66, 95, 132
Pinkertons, the, 72
Plato, 124
Pollard, Sidney, 29, 116
Power over (theory of leadership), 130
Power with (theory of leadership), 130, 133
Pre-modern, 2, 4, 5, 127, 132, 138
Principles of Scientific Management, 27, 63, 65–68, 98
Progressivism, 79, 96

Q
Quadruple Bottom Line, 136

R
Regularity of work, 79, 80
Regulatory environmentalism, 31
Republican Party, 49
Ricardo, David, 119
Rio de Janeiro, 30
Robbins, Stephen, 18, 20, 27, 28, 30, 31
Rockefeller, John D., 50
Romans, 20, 27, 96
Roosevelt, Franklin D., 50, 53, 86
Roosevelt, Theodore D., 44, 49–54, 64, 66, 85, 95, 107, 128, 132
Rousseau, Jean-Jacques, 121, 123, 125
Rowntree, Seebohm, 94

S
Samuelson, Paul A., 116

Schmidt (worker called), 27, 111
Scientific management, 9, 27, 46–48, 56–61, 63, 66–69, 76, 78, 90–94, 96–99, 106, 108–111, 113, 129, 133
Scientific Management and the Railroads, 59, 68, 69, 98, 110
Scottish Enlightenment, 119, 126
Second Earth Summit, 30
Self-interest, 73, 117, 119–122
Self-love, 121–126
Shell, 31
Simon, Herbert, 23
Slavery, 73
Smith, Adam, 25, 27, 28, 40, 84, 96, 114–129, 132, 135, 136, 138
Socialization, 124, 126
Social procurement, 80, 134
Social responsibility, 32
Special interests (of big business), 50, 54, 56, 66, 79, 80
Spencer, Herbert, 84
Spreckley, Freer, 31
Stannard Baker, Raymond, 63
Strum, Philippa, 54–56, 59, 78, 82, 85, 93
Sumerians, 20, 27
Supreme Court, 81, 86, 87, 92, 108
Sustainability, 2, 4, 5, 8, 9, 16, 18, 30–32, 35, 40, 41, 51, 98, 107, 114, 135, 136, 138
Sustainable development, 18, 30, 32, 51, 135–137
Sustainable Development Goals (SDGs), 135–137
Sympathy, sympathetic, 121–124, 126, 132

T
Taft, William H., 54
Taylor, Frederick Winslow, 9, 27–29, 40–42, 45–48, 57, 58, 61, 63–68, 90, 92–98, 107–111, 113, 114, 117, 127, 129, 132, 133, 138
Textbooks, 16–20, 23, 27, 29–34, 51, 72, 94, 96, 97, 99, 115–117, 119, 120, 129, 132, 136
The New State, 128
The Theory of Moral Sentiments, 114, 116, 120, 122, 125, 126
The Wealth of Nations, 116, 118, 123, 132
This Changes Everything, 4, 5
Tobin, John, 78
Toffler, Alvin, 33
Triple Bottom Line (TBL), 30, 31, 33, 34, 136

U
Unions, 55, 56, 71, 78–80, 115
United Nations, 18, 30, 135, 137
University of Glasgow, 125
Urwick, Lyndall F., 21, 22, 28, 29, 93–96, 129

V
Valentine, Robert G., 90, 113
Vanderbilt, Cornelius, 50
Victorian Traditional Owner Cultural Fire Strategy, 2
Vitruvius, 22
Voltaire, 121

W
Waldo, Dwight, 22
Walker, Francis Amasa, 72
Warren, Samuel, 70, 71, 74
Waru paintings, 3
Well-being, 20, 34, 50, 55, 74, 86, 94, 98, 106, 107, 128
Wendell Holmes, Oliver, 82

Wilson, Woodrow, 85–87
World War I, 45, 93
World War II, 23
Wren, Daniel A., 17, 28, 29, 67, 93, 95–97, 116, 119

Z
Zionism, 85

The manufacturer's authorised representative in the EU is Springer Nature Customer Service Centre GmbH, Europaplatz 3, 69115 Heidelberg, Germany. If you have any concerns regarding our products, please contact ProductSafety@springernature.com

Printed and bound by CPI Group (UK) Ltd, Croydon, CR0 4YY
30/09/2026
02225666-0012